I0817550

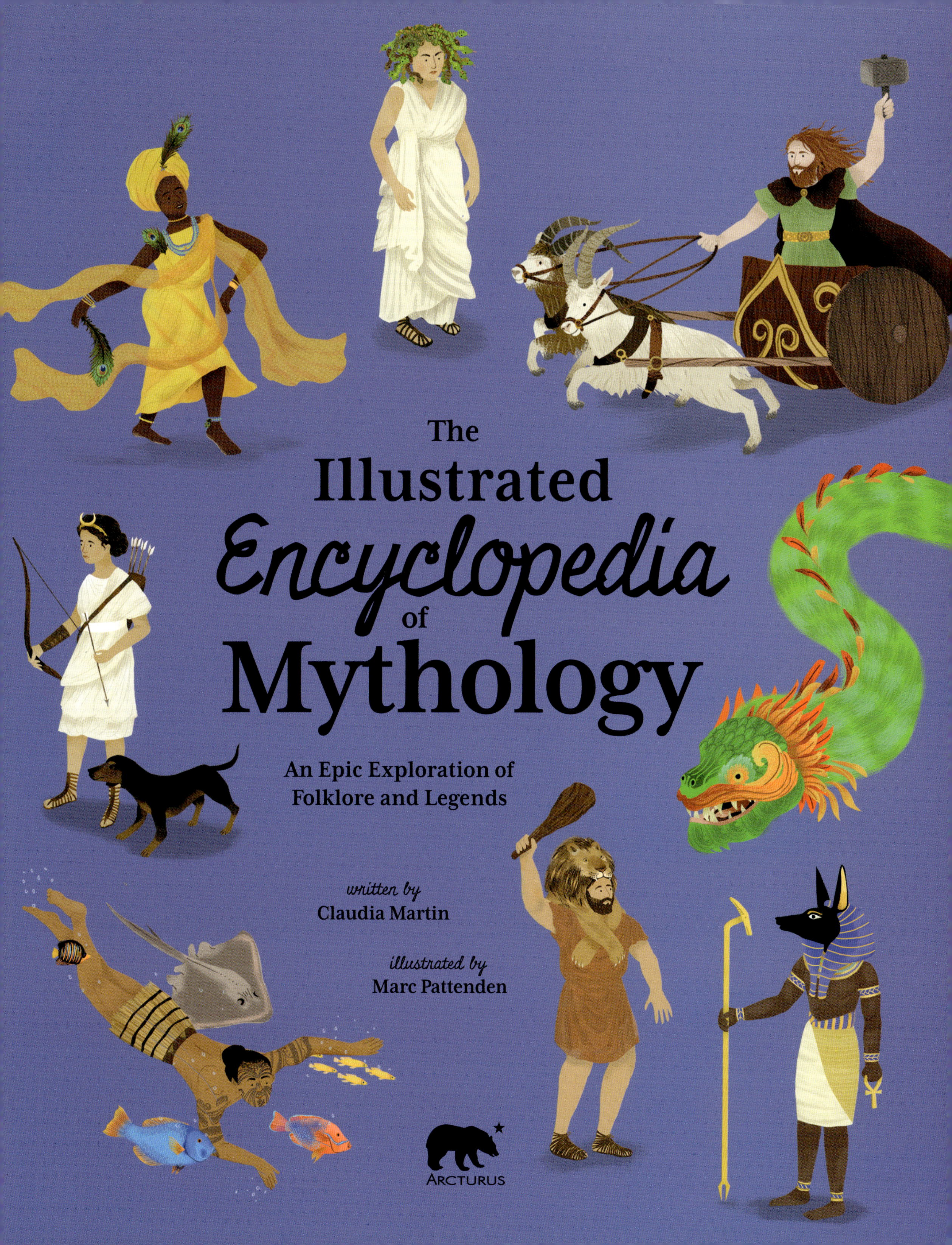
The
Illustrated
Encyclopedia
of
Mythology
An Epic Exploration of
Folklore and Legends
written by
Claudia Martin
illustrated by
Marc Pattenden
ARCTURUS

The myths in this book belong to the peoples who passed them down from generation to generation. The author and illustrator have retold and represented them here with gratitude.

This edition published in 2025 by Arcturus Publishing Limited
26/27 Bickels Yard, 151–153 Bermondsey Street,
London SE1 3HA

Author: Claudia Martin
Illustrator: Marc Pattenden
Designer: Amy McSimpson
Consultant: Philip Steele
Editor: Becca Clunes
Editorial Manager: Joe Harris
Managing Designer: Georgina Wood

ISBN: 978-1-3988-6371-2
CH011579US
Supplier 29, Date 0725, PI 00011773

Printed in China

Contents

Miraculous Mythology

Since the nights when our ancestors first clustered around a fire, humans have told each other myths. Myths are stories that pass on important facts about the world, both the world that can be seen with human eyes and the world that cannot be seen. We cannot see the forces that make the wind blow and the stars move across our sky, the forces that shaped the mountains and our planet itself, but we know that they must exist.

For most ancient peoples—and for many people today—those invisible forces were made by gods, goddesses, or spirits. Ancient peoples expressed this belief in their myths. Modern science has other explanations for these forces, which may lead some readers to feel that the myths in this book are not "true." Yet, if we look beneath the surface of many myths, they give us deeper truths about our relationships with each other and with nature.

From the beginning and across the world, all myths have had one main purpose: to awaken us. For those who believe in the gods and goddesses, myths awaken from the troubles of daily life by telling of the marvels that the gods can perform. Myths remind believers of the spiritual path they must take to move nearer to the gods. For those who do not believe in the gods and goddesses, myths are a journey away from the present, into a miraculous world where all things are possible. For both believers and non-believers, myths remind us that the most important forces in the world—love, hope, friendship—cannot be seen.

The Hindu goddess Lakshmi shows believers the way to spiritual happiness. Her four arms represent four goals: *dharma* (being kind), *kama* (being loving), *artha* (finding purpose), and *moksha* (reaching freedom through spiritual growth).

The earliest myth that has survived to today in written form is about the hero-king Gilgamesh. It was recorded on clay tablets from around 2000 BCE, in Mesopotamia, which lay in today's Iraq. Among Gilgamesh's many adventures was his battle with the Bull of Heaven, which was sent to attack him by the goddess Inanna.

What Are Myths?

Myths are traditional stories, passed from person to person over many generations. Yet myths are different from other types of stories, because they are about gods and goddesses. Myths are important to the people who tell them, because they pass on important beliefs.

RELIGIOUS STORIES

For each group of people—from the ancient Egyptians to the Aztecs—their myths grew from their religious and spiritual beliefs. Myths are about the doings of gods, goddesses, and other supernatural beings. Humans often make an appearance in myths, but they are not usually the main focus, unless it is a human so extraordinary that they become a god or goddess as reward for their actions.

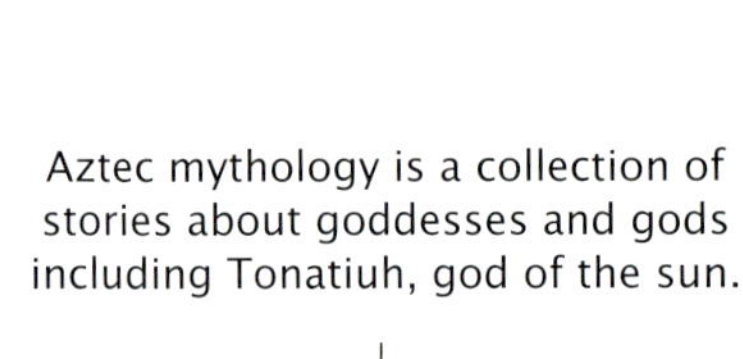

Aztec mythology is a collection of stories about goddesses and gods including Tonatiuh, god of the sun.

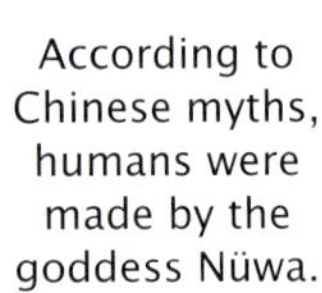

According to Chinese myths, humans were made by the goddess Nüwa.

EXPLAINING THE WORLD

As well as passing on religious beliefs, many myths explain why the world is how it is. They give us reasons for natural happenings such as seasons, earthquakes, and storms. They answer the biggest questions of all—how was the universe created and where did humans come from?

The Japanese moon god Tsukuyomi punished those who broke social rules. He was punished himself after killing one of his sisters—he was forbidden from being near the sun.

TEACHING US

Myths also teach us the rules we should obey to live happily with each other and with nature. Some rules are different in different parts of the world, such as not walking on thin Arctic sea ice or not thoughtlessly cutting down New Zealand's forests. Other rules—about kindness and respect—are the same for myth-tellers across the world.

PASSED DOWN

Myths were first told orally: as spoken stories, chanted poems, or songs. For many mythologies, it was hundreds or even thousands of years before anyone wrote down a myth. By that time, there were often many versions of each myth. Sometimes, the first people to write down a myth were outsiders—people who did not believe it was "true." Particularly in these cases, the writers put their own slant on each myth, so we can only wonder about the original story.

Christian monks were the first to write down the myths of the ancient Irish religion. In keeping with their own beliefs, the monks described the Irish goddess called The Morrigan as a fairy or witch.

SHARED STORIES

As you read this book, you may notice that myths from different corners of the world share similar ideas, including huge snakes and towering trees. Many mythologies feature an all-powerful sky god and an earth goddess. In some cases, these similarities between mythologies—such as those of the ancient Greeks and Slavs—are because they grew in the same region, from the same religious roots. In other cases, these shared stories may be due to the shared hopes, fears, and beliefs of humans across the world.

Many mythologies have trickster figures, such as the Greek Prometheus, Norse Loki, Māori Māui, and Raven (pictured) of Canada's Haida people. Tricksters play tricks on the gods, often giving forbidden gifts—such as the fire stolen by Raven—to humans.

The World of Myths

Across the world, over thousands of years, every group of people developed its own mythology. While some mythologies are well known to us, others have been forgotten or can only be partly glimpsed. The myths in this book are a selection of the world's most wonderful myths.

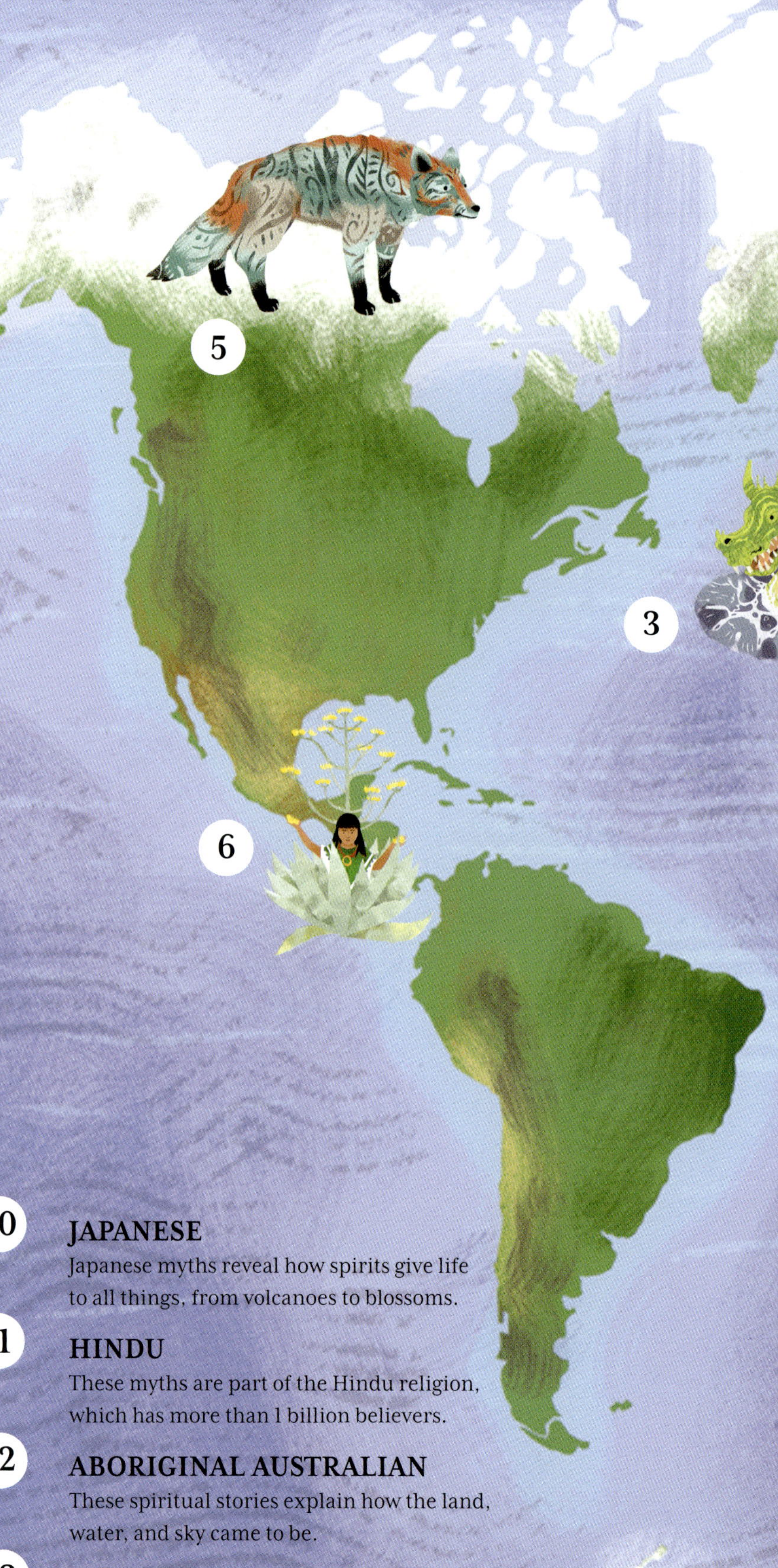

1 **GREEK**
Ancient Greek myths are tales of gods, goddesses, heroes, and fabulous creatures.

2 **NORSE**
These myths tell of battles between gods, elves, dwarves, and strange spirits.

3 **IRISH**
These stories of fierce creatures and brave gods were told in Ireland from around 500 BCE.

4 **SLAVIC**
Slavic myths, as well as fairy tales of witches and firebirds, grew from the region's ancient religion.

5 **INUIT**
Inuit stories tell of the gods, goddesses, and spirits of the far north.

6 **AZTEC**
Aztec myths reveal truths about Mexican beliefs and lives before the arrival of Europeans in the Americas.

7 **EGYPTIAN**
This mythology grew in ancient Egypt, which flourished from around 3100 to 30 BCE.

8 **YORUBA**
The Yoruba religion grew up in West Africa, but has shaped beliefs in the Americas.

9 **CHINESE**
Many Chinese myths tell of gods and spirits that take the form of all-powerful dragons.

10 **JAPANESE**
Japanese myths reveal how spirits give life to all things, from volcanoes to blossoms.

11 **HINDU**
These myths are part of the Hindu religion, which has more than 1 billion believers.

12 **ABORIGINAL AUSTRALIAN**
These spiritual stories explain how the land, water, and sky came to be.

13 **MĀORI**
Māori myths tell of the *atua* who shaped the islands of New Zealand.

2
4
1
9
10
7
11
8
12
13

Greek Mythology

In their temples and homes, the ancient Greeks worshipped twelve major gods and goddesses known as the Olympians. These gods ruled from their home on Mount Olympus, the highest mountain in Greece. The Olympians included the king of the gods, Zeus; four of his brothers and sisters; and six of his children. The twelfth Olympian was Aphrodite, goddess of love, who was born when the blood of the ancient sky god, Uranus, fell into the ocean. A thirteenth major god, named Hades, lived in the underworld and ruled the dead. In addition to these thirteen deities, the Greeks worshipped many minor gods and goddesses, from god of wine Dionysus to goddess of dawn Eos.

Greek myths were being told by singers and poet performers by 1800 BCE or even earlier. The stories were first written down by Greek poets such as Homer and Hesiod in the 8th century BCE. The myths that have been passed down to us tell the adventures of gods, goddesses, nature spirits such as nymphs, and mortal heroes and heroines.

Historians believe that the Greek myths grew from earlier stories, some told in Europe and others from western Asia or Egypt. From Greece, those stories spread to Rome, in today's Italy. The Romans, who controlled much of Europe by the 2nd century CE, adopted everything they liked about Greek religion and mythology. They identified their own gods with the Greek gods, linking Zeus with Jupiter and Aphrodite with Venus. It is the Roman versions of many Greek myths that we are telling today.

One of the most popular heroes was Heracles, whose adventures included killing a three-headed giant and a poison-breathed swamp monster. The son of Zeus and a mortal woman named Alcmene, he was made a god for his bravery.

Aphrodite was the Greek goddess of love and beauty. Her symbols—the animals and objects linked with her—were doves, seashells, and mirrors. Her children included the winged god Eros, who shot arrows at gods and humans to make them fall in love.

Children of Cronus

The cruel god Cronus was leader of the Titans, the first generation of gods to rule the world. Cronus had six children: three sons and three daughters. These children defeated the Titans in a ten-year war, then ruled from palaces on Mount Olympus, becoming the first Olympian gods.

POSEIDON

Poseidon was god of the sea, earthquakes, and horses. He carried a three-pronged fishing spear, called a trident. By striking his trident on rock, he made springs of fresh water. Poseidon fathered many children, including the heroes Bellerophon and Theseus (see page 21) and the monster Charybdis (see page 20).

HESTIA

Hestia was goddess of the home and hearth, the place in a home where a fire was kept for heating and cooking. She was remembered during sacrifices to any god or goddess, since she also ruled over temple fires, where a portion of animal sacrifices was burned.

DEMETER

The goddess of farming and harvest, Demeter was sometimes depicted carrying a sickle, which was a farming tool for cutting crops. Her sacred plant was the poppy, which grew wild among the fields of grain.

ZEUS

Zeus was the youngest of Cronus's children, but led his brothers and sisters in the war against the Titans. He became king of the Olympians and had many children of his own, some of them gods and others heroes. Zeus was god of the sky and thunder.

Zeus Fact Box

MOTHER	Rhea, a Titan daughter of the earth goddess Gaia and sky god Uranus
FATHER	Cronus, brother of Rhea, who killed Uranus and was first to rule the world
POWERS	Zeus controlled the weather, summoning storms when angry and throwing lightning bolts to destroy enemies. He could also change shape, taking the form of animals or humans to walk among mortals.

HERA

Queen of the Olympians, Hera married her brother Zeus. She was goddess of women, marriage, and family. Like her brothers and sisters—except Zeus, who was saved by his mother—Hera was swallowed by Cronus on the day she was born. Zeus forced Cronus to vomit his siblings.

HADES

The owner of a helmet that gave its wearer invisibility, Hades was god of the dead. Since he lived in a palace in the underworld, the dark home of souls after death, he was not counted among the twelve Olympian gods.

Amazing Adventures

Some of the most exciting Greek myths told of mortal heroes and heroines who battled against monsters. These heroes were either extraordinary humans or demi-gods, the children of a mortal and a god.

By killing monsters, mythological heroes and heroines showed what human bravery and cleverness can achieve. We can say that the monsters represented human fears, from natural disasters to disease and death. When a hero defeated a monster, the listeners—and, later, the readers—must have felt joy.

As well as showing the possibilities of human achievement, myths of heroes and heroines also did the opposite: They showed listeners the lines that they must not cross. At the end of many myths, the hero or heroine was punished, for sins such as pride or ingratitude. Since life for most listeners was short and difficult, there was perhaps comfort in knowing that even the best and bravest must suffer.

HERACLES

The goddess Hera was angered by the birth of Heracles, who was the son of Zeus and a mortal princess. Hera forced Heracles to perform twelve tasks, conquering monsters from a lion with gold fur to birds that shot bronze feathers.

PERSEUS

This hero killed Medusa, a snake-haired monster who turned humans to stone with her stare. Using a shiny shield lent by Athena, Perseus fought Medusa while watching only her reflection, saving himself from becoming a statue.

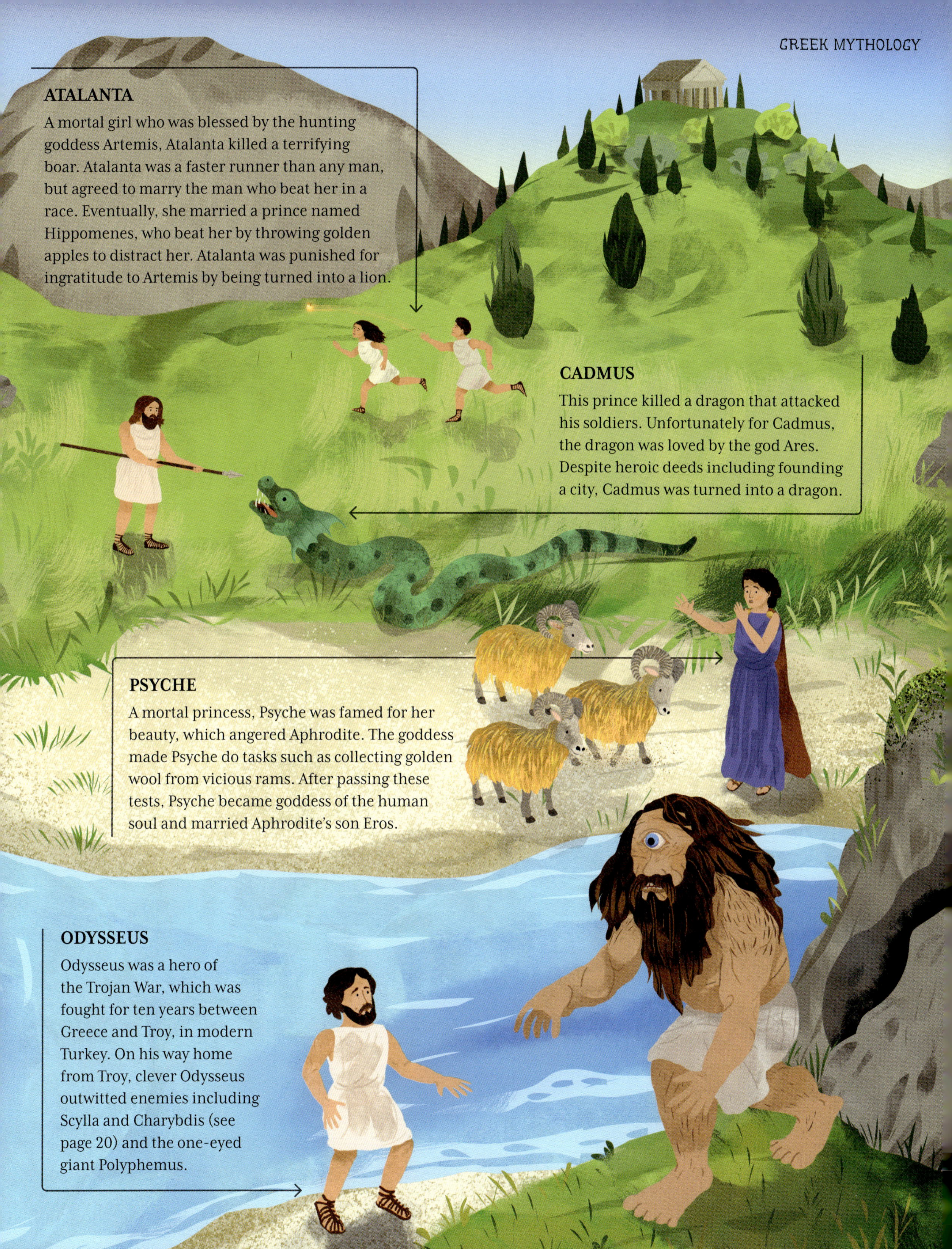

ATALANTA

A mortal girl who was blessed by the hunting goddess Artemis, Atalanta killed a terrifying boar. Atalanta was a faster runner than any man, but agreed to marry the man who beat her in a race. Eventually, she married a prince named Hippomenes, who beat her by throwing golden apples to distract her. Atalanta was punished for ingratitude to Artemis by being turned into a lion.

CADMUS

This prince killed a dragon that attacked his soldiers. Unfortunately for Cadmus, the dragon was loved by the god Ares. Despite heroic deeds including founding a city, Cadmus was turned into a dragon.

PSYCHE

A mortal princess, Psyche was famed for her beauty, which angered Aphrodite. The goddess made Psyche do tasks such as collecting golden wool from vicious rams. After passing these tests, Psyche became goddess of the human soul and married Aphrodite's son Eros.

ODYSSEUS

Odysseus was a hero of the Trojan War, which was fought for ten years between Greece and Troy, in modern Turkey. On his way home from Troy, clever Odysseus outwitted enemies including Scylla and Charybdis (see page 20) and the one-eyed giant Polyphemus.

Children of Zeus

Six of Zeus's many children were important gods and goddesses who were counted among the twelve Olympians and ruled creation from their palaces on Mount Olympus. The mothers of these Olympians were nymphs or Olympian and Titan goddesses.

ARTEMIS

Artemis was goddess of hunting, wild animals, nature, and childcare. She was the twin sister of Apollo and daughter of the Titan goddess Leto. Along with her band of nymphs, Artemis loved to hunt among forests and mountains.

APOLLO

The most beautiful of the gods, Apollo ruled over many different areas of human life, including music, dance, poetry, archery, and healing. As god of prophecy, he told the future to the priestess of the Temple of Apollo at Delphi, in central Greece.

HERMES

Hermes' mother was the nymph Maia, a daughter of the Titan Atlas who was forced to carry the sky on his shoulders by Zeus. Hermes was the messenger of the gods, able to travel fast using his winged sandals. He was the protector of human wayfarers, sailors, merchants, and thieves.

ARES

Ares was god of war, bravery, and strength. While his half-sister Athena represented the planning and leadership needed for war, Ares often represented war's cruelty and savagery. Like Hephaestus, Ares was the son of Zeus and his sister-wife Hera.

HEPHAESTUS

God of fire and volcanoes, Hephaestus also had responsibility for metalworking, carpentry, and sculpture. His symbols were tools of metalworking: a hammer, anvil, and tongs. He was known for making clockwork machines, including a gold dog and a bronze soldier.

Athena Fact Box

MOTHER	Metis, a water nymph and daughter of the Titans Oceanus and Tethys
FATHER	Zeus, from whose head Athena was born after he tricked Metis into turning into a fly and swallowed her
POWERS	Zeus's most beloved child, Athena was one of the most powerful Olympians. She guided heroes, inspired inventors and craftspeople, and gave courage to soldiers.

ATHENA

Athena was goddess of wisdom, warfare, and weaving. Her symbols included an owl, which represented wisdom, and a shield that displayed the head of Medusa (see page 14), who was killed by Perseus with Athena's guidance. The goddess protected cities including Athens, which took her name.

Persephone

The goddess Demeter had a daughter named Persephone, whose hair was as brown as the soil, her eyes as green as new shoots. The goddess of farming loved Persephone more than she loved golden ears of barley, more than she loved the scarlet poppies that grew among the crops. Demeter kept Persephone close by her side, for fear that another god's jealousy—or love—would take her away.

One sun-washed afternoon, as Persephone picked windflowers in her mother's fields, she heard a low whisper: "Persephone! Persephone!"

"Who's there?" cried Persephone, turning to see a tall man in a black cloak, his forehead furrowed with creases.

"I am Hades, king of the underworld. Would you like to visit my kingdom?" asked that dark god, who longed to have bright Persephone as his companion.

Persephone had heard tales of the underworld, that deep, dismal place where pale-faced souls spent eternity in Hades' strict care. "I should like to see the three-headed guard dog Cerberus," said Persephone excitedly.

With a stamp of his foot, Hades shook open a crack in the ground. Persephone disappeared into the earth.

"Persephone!" cried Demeter, when she could not see her daughter. "Persephone!" she cried as she ran through the fields. As dreadful night followed day, as month followed month, Demeter wandered across earth's surface in search of her daughter. As Demeter wept and begged for a glimpse of her child, she forgot to care for the earth.

Seeds did not grow. Buds did not open. Vines did not stretch and spread.

Helios, god of the sun, saw leaves falling to the hard ground. He saw children hungering. He called: "Demeter, I see all from my perch. Your daughter went with Hades."

Her heart fluttering with hope, Demeter sent her nephew Hermes to the underworld. On his winged sandals, Hermes flew fast through those dim caverns to Hades' candlelit palace.

There sat Persephone on a golden throne beside the onyx throne of Hades. In the goddess's hand was a pomegranate, from which she plucked seeds as bright as rubies.

"Persephone, you must return to your mother," said Hermes, "for without your love, she has left all the world's plants to die."

Persephone sprang to her feet. "Husband," she cried to Hades, for she had married that stern god, "I must return to the land of the living."

"My love," answered Hades, his voice cracking with sadness, "you have eaten food in my kingdom, so you cannot leave."

"Six seeds," gasped Persephone, staring at the fruit in her hand. "I ate only six seeds in all this time. Let me go to my mother, who needs me as much as you."

Hades nodded grimly. "Since you ate six seeds, you must spend six months of each year with me, then six months with your mother."

Taking leave of her husband, Persephone rushed into the sunlight, where Demeter hugged her and held her tight. At once, green shoots poked through the soil, thickened, and grew tall. Bees buzzed from blossom to blossom.

When mother and daughter had spent six blooming months together, Persephone returned to the underworld. For the next six months, Demeter let her plants shrink into the cold soil. And that is what has happened ever since, with winter following summer as surely as spring always returns, just like Persephone.

Persephone Fact Box

MOTHER	Demeter, goddess of farming
FATHER	Zeus, king of the gods
POWERS	As goddess of spring, Persephone made seeds and new shoots grow each year. As goddess of the underworld, she also made plants die back, disappearing into the earth, each winter.

Animals and Monsters

Strange animals and monsters appear in many Greek myths. Storytellers used these creatures to explain why the world contained dangers such as whirlpools and storms. Greek monsters were often a mix of two familiar animals or a combination of human and animal.

CERBERUS

This dog guarded the gate of the Underworld of the Dead, stopping the dead from escaping to the land of the living. Cerberus is often described as having three heads and a tail ending in a snake's head.

HIPPOCAMPUS

Half-horse and half-fish, this creature's name comes from the ancient Greek *hippos* (meaning "horse") and *campos* (meaning "sea monster"). The chariot of the sea god Poseidon was pulled by a team of these seahorses.

SCYLLA AND CHARYBDIS

These monsters lived on either side of the narrow sea channel between the island of Sicily and the Italian mainland. Scylla had six hungry mouths, but Charybdis was the more dangerous of the two monsters: She sucked and spewed water to make whirlpools that wrecked ships.

HARPY

The harpies were women with the wings and claws of birds. Vicious and violent, the harpies were the spirits of storm winds. They snatched possessions and people, carrying them into the air in their sharp claws.

MINOTAUR

The ferocious Minotaur had the body of a man, but the head and tail of a bull. It was imprisoned in a maze, called the Labyrinth, by King Minos of Crete. Minos fed the Minotaur with unwilling humans, until the monster was killed by the hero Theseus.

PEGASUS

This flying horse was tamed by the hero Bellerophon, who rode him into battle against the fire-breathing monster Chimera. Afterward, Pegasus lived with Zeus and carried the god's thunderbolts and lightning.

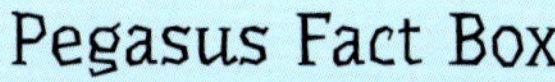

Pegasus Fact Box

MOTHER	Medusa, a snake-haired monster who turned humans to stone with her stare
FATHER	Poseidon, god of the sea, earthquakes, and horses
POWERS	When Pegasus's hooves kicked the ground, water spurted from the rock, creating springs such as the Hippocrene on Mount Helicon. Drinking this spring's water gave people the ability to write poetry.

Pandora's Jar

The first humans were all men, with not a woman among them. They lived safely in the garden that Zeus made for them. They knew neither disease nor death, sickness nor sadness, since Zeus's creation did not hold those troubles. Then—against Zeus's wishes, against his orders—the men accepted the gift of fire from the mischievous Titan named Prometheus. Zeus decided to punish those first men—and every human who would ever live.

"Hephaestus!" cried Zeus. "Make a woman to live among the men. I want her to take a gift to those disobedient humans."

"The first woman!" gasped Hephaestus. "I will model her on Aphrodite, the most beautiful of all goddesses."

Hephaestus set to work with sticky clay. As he squeezed and rolled, three goddesses came into his workshop. When Hephaestus's clay had taken the shape of a woman, the first of the goddesses stepped forward.

It was Hera, queen of the gods. "Before you give life to the woman, we must give her gifts." She pressed her hands onto the woman's damp clay chest. "I give her kindness."

The second goddess waved her bow and arrows. It was Artemis, goddess of hunting. "I give her bravery."

The last goddess strode forward. It was Athena, goddess of wisdom. "I give her curiosity, the desire to learn and discover."

Prometheus Fact Box

MOTHER	Clymene, the Titan goddess of fame
FATHER	Iapetus, a Titan son of the earth goddess Gaia and sky god Uranus
POWERS	Prometheus had great intelligence and cunning. He stole fire from the gods and gave it to the first men, allowing humankind to progress, invent, and discover.

"We will call her Pandora," said Hephaestus, "which means 'all gifts.'"

Then Hephaestus called the four winds, which blew into the clay woman's nostrils until she breathed and became skin, hair, and pearly nails. Pandora's eyes opened wide with wonder.

Now Zeus came into the workshop. He gave Pandora a lidded jar that was painted with twisting serpents. "Take this jar to the men in the garden. Yet, whatever you do, you must never lift the jar's lid."

All went as Zeus expected. The men welcomed Pandora. She soon shared their gentle work as they plucked fruit from the heavy branches of fig and apple trees.

The men turned their faces away from Pandora's jar, since they did not dare disobey Zeus a second time. Yet Pandora found her face always turned to that jar. As the sun rose and set, as the moon grew and shrank, Pandora itched with curiosity to know what was in the jar.

When Pandora could not bear the not-knowing any longer, she snatched the jar and crept out of sight. She drew a deep breath, then lifted the lid.

Dark wings flapped from the jar, slapping Pandora's face.

"I am sadness!" cried the flapping thing as it soared into the shivering air. "I am sickness!" wailed a second dark creature as it burst from the jar. "I am disease!" hissed a third. "I am death!" screamed a fourth.

Pandora cried out: "Oh, what have I done?"

Then a little voice whispered, just loudly enough for Pandora to hear: "Now those evils are in the world, there is nothing you can do to stop them. They will make humans weep for ever more. Yet, if you hold me close, I will help."

A tiny creature fluttered from the jar. Its wings were delicate as petals laden with morning dew.

"What are you?" asked Pandora, letting the precious creature perch on her finger.

"I am hope," it answered.

Norse Mythology

The Norse myths tell the stories of gods and goddesses who belonged to two groups: the Aesir and Vanir. The Aesir lived in a heavenly world named Asgard, which—after a war between the two clans—also became home to the Vanir. There was a third group of gods, or godlike beings, named the Jötnar. The Jötnar are often called "giants" or "trolls" in English, yet they were of ordinary size and might be either monstrous or beautiful. The Jötnar lived in a world named Jotunheim or in wild places such as mountains. They were often enemies of the Aesir and Vanir, but were sometimes their parents, lovers, and friends.

In addition to the gods and goddesses, other supernatural beings make an appearance in Norse myths. These include elves, which were shining and beautiful; and dwarves, which were linked with the earth and metalwork. The valkyries were female spirits who guided the souls of the dead.

Norse myths grew up in Scandinavia—the region of modern Norway, Sweden, and Denmark—in the many centuries before Scandinavians became Christians. The myths spread to other parts of northern Europe, such as Iceland, that were conquered by Scandinavian warriors and farmers, who are often known as Vikings. As Christianity replaced the Old Norse religion between the 8th and 12th centuries, the old stories continued to be told. Many myths were first written down in the 13th century, in a collection of poems called the *Poetic Edda*, and in a textbook called the *Prose Edda*, which was probably the work of an Icelandic historian named Snorri Sturluson.

One of the Jötnar, Skadi was goddess of mountains, winter, skiing, and hunting with a bow. She married Njördr, the Vanir god of the sea. The marriage failed, since Skadi hated the sea and Njördr hated mountains.

The sun goddess, Sól, rides her chariot through the sky every day, chased by a wolf named Sköll. Sól's brother Máni, god of the moon, is chased by a wolf named Hati Hródvitnisson. This will continue until the time of Ragnarök, the end of the current worlds, when the wolves will swallow the sun and moon.

Aesir and Vanir

Most of the major Norse gods and goddesses were members of the Aesir and Vanir clans. The myths tell us how these gods fought, loved, and tricked each other. They created the worlds and usually battled against the forces of chaos that threatened to destroy them.

ODIN

Leader of the Aesir, this god helped to create the worlds (see page 30). As god of wisdom, Odin sacrificed an eye to see everything that happens, while his two ravens brought him news. As god of war, Odin ruled Valhalla, the hall in Asgard where half of all warriors killed in battle were brought by his helpers, the valkyries.

FRIGG

The goddess of marriage and motherhood, Frigg was the wife of Odin and queen of the Aesir. She could see into the future, yet never told anyone what she saw. The English word Friday comes from the Old English words for "Frigg's Day."

GEFJON

This Aesir goddess was associated with plowing, which she did with the help of her four sons, who were oxen. Her plow cut the earth so deeply, drawing it out into the sea, that she created the Danish island of Zealand.

FREYR

Along with his twin sister Freyja, Freyr was a member of the Vanir. He was god of peace, fine weather, good harvest, wealth, and kings. He owned a sword that fought on its own, but he gave it away in order to marry the beautiful Gerdr, a member of the Jötnar. His boar, named Gullinbursti, had gold bristles that glowed in the dark.

THOR

One of the most popular gods among the Vikings, Thor was god of thunder, lightning, storms, and strength. His chariot was pulled by two goats, which Thor ate and then brought back to life using his hammer, named Mjölnir. The English day of the week Thursday is named for Thor.

FREYJA

Freyja was the goddess of love, beauty, and magic. She received half of the warriors killed in battle, hosting them in her hall. Freyja owned a cloak of falcon feathers, which gave its wearer the ability to fly. She also drove a chariot pulled by two cats.

Thor Fact Box

MOTHER	Jörd, the Aesir goddess of the earth
FATHER	Odin, king of the Aesir
POWERS	The strongest of the Aesir, Thor used his heavy hammer to kill enemies and shatter mountains. When Thor threw the hammer, it always hit his target then returned to his hand.

"Loki! Only you could have committed such a crime!" shouted Thor when he saw Sif's shorn head. His voice thundered through Asgard, shaking the branches of the world tree.

Loki knew that, wherever he hid, Thor's fist would break his bones. So he hurried to Asgard, where he faced the scowling gods Thor, Odin, and Freyr.

"Do not fret," simpered Loki. "I will bring a new head of hair for Sif." Then he darted away, not stopping until he reached Nidavellir, home of the dwarves.

In those dark and dripping caves, Loki found the Sons of Ivaldi, their hammers throwing shimmering sparks as they shaped iron. Loki told the dwarves that he needed a cap of golden hair, as well as gifts for Odin and Freyr. "I shall pay you with all the gold in Asgard," he lied.

At once, Brokkr and Eitri set to work on a piece of gold. Yet, Loki transformed himself into a fly and bit Brokkr's hand, making the dwarf drop the gold into the fire. Now that gold was shaped into a gold-bristled boar named Gullinbursti, who could run faster than any horse. "That gift is for Freyr," grumbled Brokkr.

As Brokkr and Eitri shaped a second piece of gold, that cunning fly bit Brokkr on the neck, so he dropped the metal into the fire. When the gold was plucked out, it was a ring named Draupnir, from which—every ninth night—dripped eight new rings. "That gift is for Odin," groaned Brokkr.

When Brokkr and Eitri hammered a piece of iron, the crafty fly bit Brokkr on the eye, so he dropped that iron into the fire. That hot metal was now a hammer named Mjölnir. "That gift is for Thor," growled Brokkr.

Loki Fact Box

MOTHER	Laufey, one of the Aesir, whose name means "leafy"
FATHER	Fárbauti, one of the Jötnar, whose name means "dangerous striker"
POWERS	Loki was a shape-shifter, able to change his form to appear as a fly, salmon, seal, horse, and old woman. A prophecy foretold that, during Ragnarök, he and his children would help to destroy the current worlds.

Yet, Loki was already running to Asgard with his six gifts. You can be sure that Sif, Thor, Odin, and Freyr were delighted. But no one had a chance to celebrate before Brokkr and Eitri stormed into the hall.

"You cannot have my head," crowed Loki, "since your gifts were made with the help of a fly."

"It was our hands that worked the metal!" roared Brokkr, pulling out his knife.

"Wait," gasped Loki, thinking fast. "I said you could have my head but never mentioned my neck. Are you sure you can take one without taking any of the other?"

Knowing they were beaten, Brokkr and Eitri stamped back to Nidavellir. And Loki used his head to think up a new trick.

Nine Worlds

In Old Norse religion, the universe was made up of nine worlds that surrounded a vast tree, named Yggdrasil. These worlds were home to different beings, with humans in Midgard and the Aesir in Asgard.

Along with his brothers Vili and Vé, the god Odin created the worlds after he killed Ymir, the first being. The brothers made earth from Ymir's flesh, mountains from his bones, trees from his hair, ocean from his blood, and the heavens from his skull.

Ymir's eyebrows were shaped into Midgard, the world where humans would live. Odin and his brothers found two tree trunks on Midgard's shore. They carved the wood into the first two humans, Ask and Embla, who became the parents of all humans.

YGGDRASIL

Several creatures lived in this vast ash tree. Nidhogg was a dragon or worm that gnawed the tree's roots. On top of the tree was a hawk named Vedrfolnir that perched between the eyes of an eagle. A squirrel named Ratatoskr carried messages between Nidhogg and Vedrfolnir.

ASGARD

Home of the Aesir gods and also, later, of the Vanir, Asgard was a walled town containing palaces and feasting halls.

MIDGARD

Home of humans, Midgard was circled by a sea in which lived a huge serpent, named Jörmungandr.

JOTUNHEIM

The home of many of the Jötnar, this land may have encircled Midgard on the opposite side of the world sea.

NIDAVELLIR

This world, with a name meaning "Dark Fields," was home to the dwarves.

MUSPELHEIM

A place of intense heat and fire, this world was home to the Jötnar of fire.

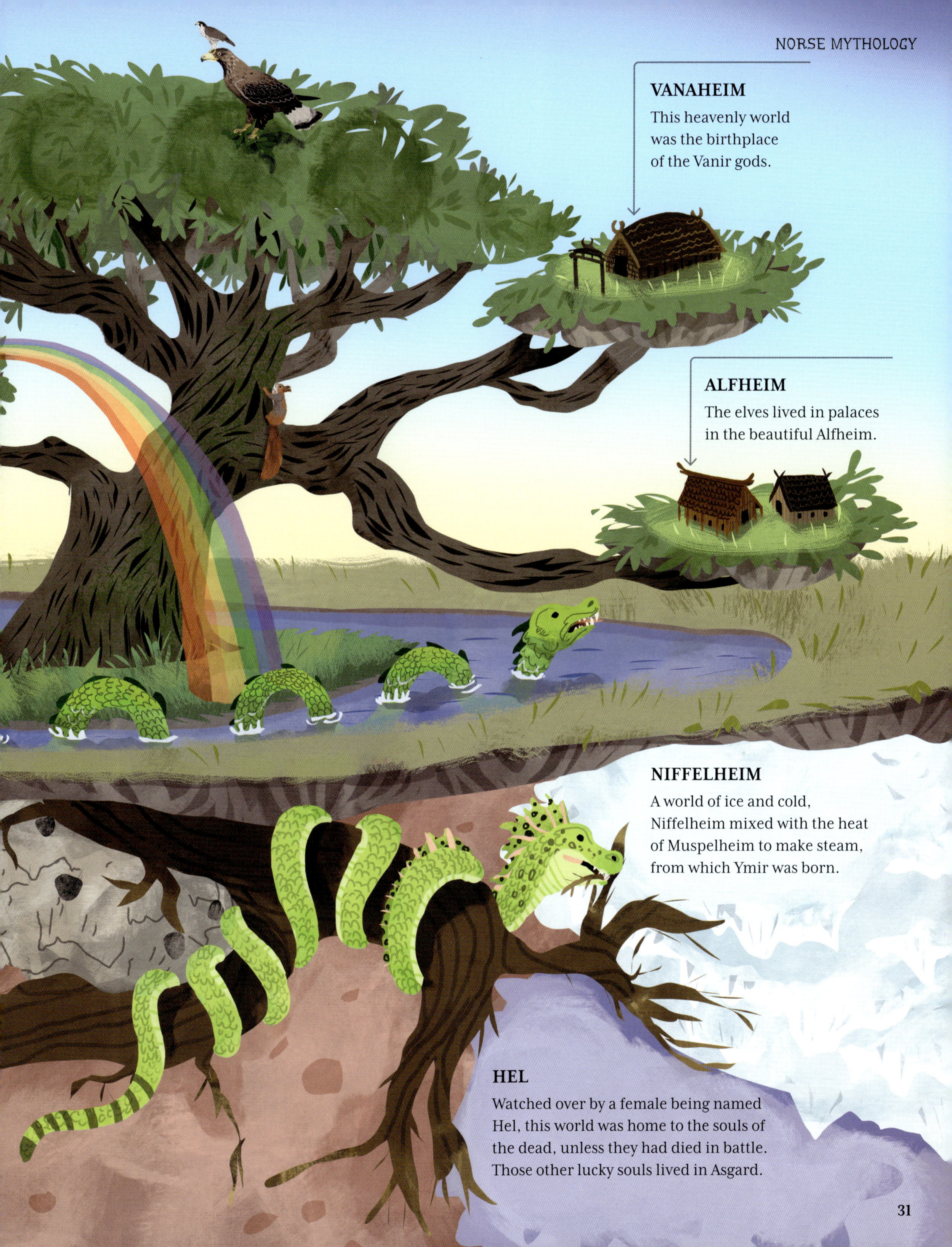

VANAHEIM

This heavenly world was the birthplace of the Vanir gods.

ALFHEIM

The elves lived in palaces in the beautiful Alfheim.

NIFFELHEIM

A world of ice and cold, Niffelheim mixed with the heat of Muspelheim to make steam, from which Ymir was born.

HEL

Watched over by a female being named Hel, this world was home to the souls of the dead, unless they had died in battle. Those other lucky souls lived in Asgard.

Binding Fenrir

In Jotunheim, in the depths of the Iron Wood, lived Angrboda. She was the bitterest being in that dismal place. Angrboda had three children, who were named Fenrir, Jörmungandr, and Hel. The father of those children was none other than Loki, bringer of chaos. When the gods heard that those three children were growing strong in Jotunheim, they knew they must act.

"A sorceress has whispered to my ravens," cried Odin to the gods and goddesses. "She has seen the future. Angrboda's children will destroy the worlds at the time of Ragnarök."

At once, the gods set out for Jotunheim. They captured those three monsters, then dragged them before Odin.

Odin spoke first to Hel, a blue-skinned giantess. "At Ragnarök, it is prophesied that you will lead an army of the dead against us." Then he threw Hel from Asgard. She landed among the roots of Yggdrasil, where she has watched over the dead ever since.

Odin spoke next to Jörmungandr, a twisting serpent with scales of glittering green. "At Ragnarök, it is prophesied you will writhe in the world sea until waves drown the land." Then he threw Jörmungandr from Asgard. He landed in the world sea, where he has swum ever since.

Odin spoke last to Fenrir, a sharp-toothed wolf cub. "At Ragnarök, you will swallow me whole." But Odin did not throw Fenrir from Asgard. He kept that wolf close by.

Only Odin's son Tyr was brave enough to throw food to Fenrir. Tyr soon noticed that the wolf grew larger every day. By the third day, he was tall as Odin's spear.

The gods agreed that, to keep Asgard safe, Fenrir must be bound. They dragged an iron chain, named Leyding, toward the snoring wolf. "Will you test your strength with this chain, Fenrir?" asked Tyr. "Let us wrap it around you, then see if you can break it."

Fenrir opened a lazy eye. "Do as you please."

Fenrir Fact Box

MOTHER	Angrboda, one of the Jötnar, whose name means "sorrow-bringer"
FATHER	Loki, a trickster god and one of the Aesir
POWERS	At Ragnarök, Fenrir's strength will snap Gleipnir so he can burn the worlds with flames from his eyes and nostrils. At the same time, his children Sköll and Hati Hródvitnisson will eat the sun and moon.

Layding was wrapped around Fenrir. With one kick, the wolf snapped that chain, then went back to sleep.

The next day, the gods brought a stronger chain, named Dromi. "Try this chain, Fenrir," said Tyr. "If you can break Dromi, your fame will never end."

Fenrir scratched behind his ear. "That chain looks stronger than the last, but I have grown stronger since yesterday, too. You may bind me."

Dromi was wrapped around Fenrir. With a stretch and a shake, the wolf snapped that chain.

Now Fenrir had grown big enough to rest his muzzle on the roof of Odin's hall. The gods' fear was growing even faster. They sent a message to the dwarves, who made a slim silken ribbon, named Gleipnir. It was made with the roots of a mountain, the sound of a cat's footsteps, and the breath of a fish.

When Fenrir saw the gods carrying Gleipnir, his fur stood on end. "Don't come near me," he growled.

"Let us strike a deal," offered Tyr. "If you can't break free from Gleipnir, we will know that we have nothing to fear from you, so we will let you wander free in the worlds."

"To be sure that you do as you promise, one of you must place your hand in my mouth while I am being bound," said Fenrir. "I'll take your hand if you take my freedom."

Tyr stepped forward, breathing heavily. He put his right hand in the wolf's jaws.

Gleipnir was wrapped around Fenrir. The wolf kicked, but the bind only tightened. The more Fenrir struggled and stretched and shook, the stronger Gleipnir grew.

Everyone cheered except Tyr, who had sacrificed his right hand. From that day to this, the gods have kept Fenrir bound. He will remain bound until Ragnarök is upon us.

Irish Mythology

Stories of gods, goddesses, heroes, and fierce creatures were told in Ireland for more than a thousand years before the tales were written down. These stories grew from the religious beliefs of peoples living in Ireland and Western Europe, from about 500 BCE, who spoke Celtic languages. It was in medieval times, from around the 10th century, that monks recorded the myths with quill pens and ink. Yet, since the monks were Christians working in a country that had now converted to Christianity, they made many changes to the tales.

The medieval monks tell us that the gods and goddesses were known as the Tuatha Dé Danann. Yet the monks were careful not to actually call them "gods" and "goddesses." The monks described the Tuatha Dé Danann as immortal, but described them more as powerful fairies than as gods. In fact, the monks described how the Tuatha Dé Danann, who had once roamed freely across Ireland, had been forced to live in the Otherworld by the arrival of humans. The Otherworld was reached by entering the ground in ancient burial mounds or caves. By describing this "burial" of the Tuatha Dé Danann, medieval writers were perhaps suggesting how ancient religious beliefs were buried by the arrival of Christianity, causing the all-powerful gods and goddesses to be spoken of only as hiding, flitting fairies.

As well as tales of the Tuatha Dé Danann, Irish mythology includes stories about another supernatural race, the Fomorians. These beings, who were often monstrous and destructive, were the enemies of the Tuatha Dé Danann. Among the most popular of the Irish stories that we know today are those of heroes such as Fionn mac Cumhaill and Cú Chulainn. These warriors were mortal but had extraordinary, superhuman powers.

The Caoránach was a human-eating, cattle-chewing water serpent. The hungry monster was born from the thigh bone of a witch after she was killed by Fionn mac Cumhaill and his band of warriors. Eventually, the monster was killed by a warrior named Conan.

A famous Irish myth is about the children of Lir, who was probably a sea god of the Tuatha Dé Danann. He had four children: a girl named Finnguala, and three sons named Aodh, Fiacra, and Conn. The children's jealous stepmother turned them into swans for 900 years. When the children regained their human form, Christianity had come to Ireland.

The Tuatha Dé Danann

Many scholars believe that Tuatha Dé Danann means "folk of the goddess Danu" in the Old Irish language. This translation suggests that these immortal beings were the children of a mother goddess named Danu, yet we know almost nothing of a goddess with that name.

THE DAGDA

The Dagda (meaning "great god" in the old Celtic language) was a king of the Tuatha Dé Danann. He held a staff, its smooth end able to bring the dead back to life, but its rough end causing instant death. He also had a cauldron that was always full of food, no matter how many people ate from it.

THE MORRIGAN

Wife of the Dagda, the Morrigan was associated with war. She often took the shape of a crow to flap over battlefields. She inspired warriors to fight bravely and warned of death or victory in battle. Some think her name comes from the old Celtic words for "great queen," while others think it means "nightmare queen."

FLIDAIS

Stories such as the *Táin Bó Cúailnge* (Cattle Raid of Cooley) tell us that Flidais owned a herd of cattle that could supply milk for a whole army. While medieval writers did not call Flidais a "goddess," it is likely she was originally a goddess of cattle and milking.

MANANNÁN

Manannán ruled over the surviving Tuatha Dé Danann after they were driven into the Otherworld. Originally a god of the sea, Manannán was said to ride his chariot over the waves or to travel in a boat that found its own way.

AENGUS

Aengus was the son of the Dagda and Boann, the goddess of the River Boyne, which flows through eastern Ireland. It is believed that Aengus was originally the god of youth, summer, and love. One story tells us that Aengus fell in love with a girl he saw in a dream, then he searched Ireland for many years before finding her.

BRIGID

The ancient Irish festival of Imbolc, which marked the beginning of spring, was linked with the goddess Brigid. Today, the festival is celebrated on St. Brigid's Day, 1 February.

It is believed that St. Brigid was a Christian woman who set up an abbey in Ireland in the 5th century. Some people think that ideas about Brigid the ancient goddess and Brigid the Christian saint became mingled during medieval times.

Brigid Fact Box

MOTHER An unknown member of the Tuatha Dé Danann

FATHER The Dagda

POWERS Brigid was associated with poetry, wisdom, metalworking, healing, newborn babies, and farm animals. For the ancient Irish, she was particularly important during the lambing season, when baby lambs are born, which began during or soon after her festival of Imbolc.

The Battle of Mag Tuired

The enemies of the Tuatha Dé Danann were the Fomorians, who were said to come from inside the earth and under the sea. The Tuatha defeated the Formorians at the Battle of Mag Tuired, which may have been the name of a plain in northwestern Ireland.

Medieval writers describe the Fomorians as having a monstrous appearance, with the heads of goats or one eye in the middle of their forehead. Yet some Fomorians, such as Bres, were described as dangerously beautiful. For the ancient Irish, the Fomorians probably represented the destructive powers of nature, from death and disease to drought and darkness—everything that could destroy the order imposed by the Tuatha Dé Danann.

To keep peace between the Tuatha Dé Danann and Fomorians, a prince of the Fomorians—Bres—married the great princess of the Tuatha, Brigid. From then on, Bres ruled over both races. Yet the cruel Fomorian made the Tuatha work as servants. After seven years of this injustice, the Tuatha rose up against the Fomorians, winning victory at Mag Tuired.

BALOR

A leader of the Fomorian army, Balor was a terrifying giant with one eye that could kill with only a look. A stone thrown by Lugh made Balor's eye shoot out of the back of his head. The eye's stare then killed many Fomorians. Balor's falling body crushed yet more of them.

LUGH

Lugh's father was Cian of the Tuatha Dé Danann, but his mother was Ethniu, daughter of the dreadful Fomorian giant named Balor. Lugh led the army of the Tuatha Dé Danann to victory, killing his own grandfather with a stone shot from his sling.

BRES

After the Fomorians' defeat, Bres was found—alone and without weapons—on the battlefield by Lugh. Bres begged for his life. Lugh agreed to let Bres live, on the condition that he taught the Tuatha Dé Danann the skills of farming.

NUADA

The first king of the Tuatha Dé Danann, Nuada had lost an arm in an earlier battle against the Fir Bolg, who lived in Ireland before the Tuatha. From then on, Nuada wore a left arm made of silver. Despite his bravery, Nuada was killed by the Fomorians at Mag Tuired.

OGMA

Ogma was a great warrior of the Tuatha Dé Danann. Along with the Dagda, he pursued the Fomorians to take back the harp Uaithne. Ogma is also said to have created Ogham, an alphabet used to write the Old Irish language.

UAITHNE

The Dagda's harp, named Uaithne, was stolen by the Fomorians as they fled the battlefield. The magic harp would not play a note unless the Dagda called it by its two names, which may have been "summer" and "winter." When the Dagda played his harp, he put the seasons in their correct order.

Fionn and the Fire-Breather

That year, as every year, the festival of Samhain would mark the start of winter. People would light bonfires and pray to the gods for help in the dark days ahead. But everyone knew that it was not just bonfires that would burn this Samhain. For, on every Samhain for the last twenty-three years, the demon named Aillen the Fire-Breather had burned the city of Tara, leaving nothing but cinders. No one—not even the king's band of Fianna warriors—had ever saved Tara from Aillen's yearly destruction.

Far from Tara, deep in the forest of the Slieve Bloom Mountains, lived a boy named Fionn mac Cumhaill. Fionn was only ten years old, but he was already as brave and wise as a warrior thrice his age. When Fionn heard of Aillen's frightening flames, he set out for Tara at once.

"Wait, Fionn," cried Fíacha mac Congha, the white-haired warrior who cared for that young boy. "You cannot defeat Aillen with your bare hands. Take my spear, which is dipped in deadly poison."

So it was that, when Fionn arrived at King Cormac's palace in Tara, he gripped a spear taller than himself. Everyone, from farmers to Fianna warriors, was crowding into the king's hall for the feast of Samhain. Fionn sidled inside with the rest, then gladly ate and drank the king's meat and mead. Outside the palace, darkness fell. Bonfires pricked into life on the hillsides.

Just as Fionn was beginning to feel full, there was a cheer. The leader of the Fianna, named Goll mac Morna, got to his feet. "King Cormac," roared that warrior, "I promise that the Fianna will defend Tara against Aillen tonight."

Before the words had died on Goll's lips, Fionn heard music floating in through the hall's open door. Someone was strumming a harp, the sound sweeter than any Fionn had dreamed. Yet with every note of the harp, Fionn felt his eyelids grow heavier. Wrenching open his eyes, he saw that everyone was falling asleep. Their heads were dropping onto each other's shoulders, onto their plates.

"The music is bewitching us into sleep! I must not sleep," cried Fionn, "or there will be no one awake to defend Tara!" At once, he sniffed his spear's poisoned tip. He choked, he coughed—but the poison had startled him awake. His throat burning, his eyes smarting, he ran outside to find the harp-player.

There stood Aillen, taller than King Cormac's highest halls, his hair red as fire and his eyes glittering with glee. A harp was clutched under Aillen's bony arm. "Tara will burn again tonight!" crowed Aillen to our lone hero. Then the Fire-Breather opened his mouth, drew a deep breath—and blew flames at Fionn.

Fionn leaped aside just in time. Aillen's flames set light to a barn, from which the cows galloped in wide-eyed panic. Fionn could smell his own singed hair.

Aillen was taking another deep breath. But Fionn readied his spear, drew his own deep breath—and hurled that spear as hard as he could.

Fionn's spear struck Aillen in the forehead. That demon swayed, tottered, and fell to the ground in a shower of sparks. The Fire-Breather was dead.

Fionn lost no time in waking King Cormac, who saw at once that Fionn would be the greatest hero that Ireland had ever known. Cormac made him leader of the Fianna, that band of warriors who always did—and always will—defend Ireland in her hour of need.

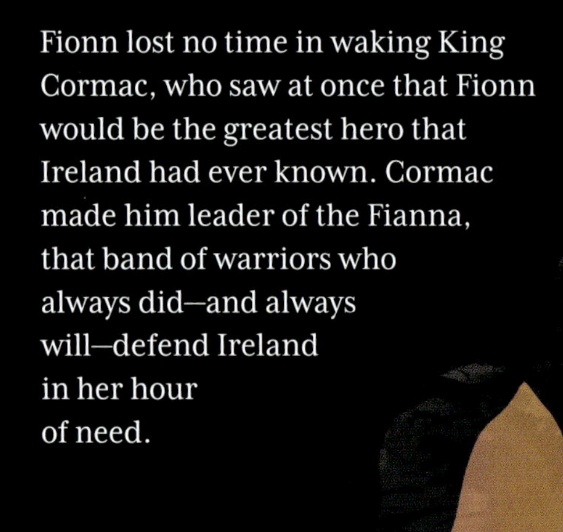

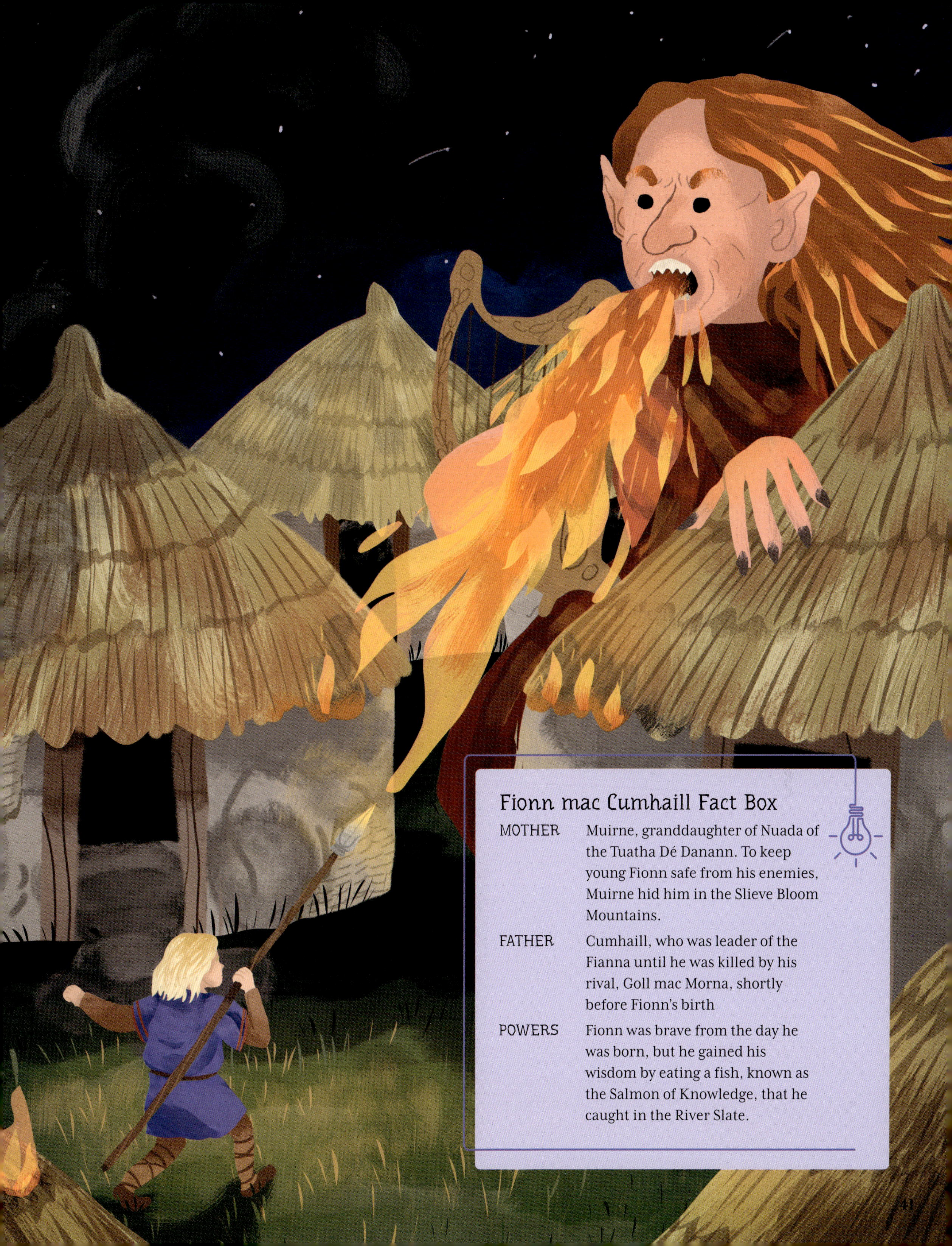

Fionn mac Cumhaill Fact Box

MOTHER	Muirne, granddaughter of Nuada of the Tuatha Dé Danann. To keep young Fionn safe from his enemies, Muirne hid him in the Slieve Bloom Mountains.
FATHER	Cumhaill, who was leader of the Fianna until he was killed by his rival, Goll mac Morna, shortly before Fionn's birth
POWERS	Fionn was brave from the day he was born, but he gained his wisdom by eating a fish, known as the Salmon of Knowledge, that he caught in the River Slate.

Slavic Mythology

Slavic mythology grew among the Slavic people, whose homeland was probably in the region of today's Poland, Belarus, and Ukraine. It was here that the Slavic religion developed and that its many gods and goddesses were first worshipped at wooden temples, on hilltops, and at festivals. As Slavic people settled farther afield—from Germany in the west to Russia in the east and Bulgaria in the south—their beliefs developed, so the myths told by eastern Slavs became different from the tales of western Slavs. For example, the creation myth told over the page comes from the Carpathian Mountains in southeastern Europe, but in a creation myth from Slovenia, the world forms from a giant egg.

We know less about Slavic mythology than about other European mythologies. The Slavic myths grew in the days before Christianity spread across the region, which happened between the 7th and 13th centuries. Yet the myths were not written down until many centuries later, in the 19th century, by which time many different myth-tellers had added their own touches. Today, we can only make guesses about the original myths, based on a scattered collection of fairy tales, songs, sayings, and customs. Our guesses are helped by details about gods, temples, and festivals that were written down by medieval visitors to the region.

Over the centuries, many Slavic myths have become a mixture of mythology and folklore. While mythology is sacred stories about gods and goddesses, folklore is not usually religious. Folklore includes songs, games, and fairy tales, which are stories for children that feature magic, fanciful creatures, and princesses. For example, we know of the firebird (see page 50) from fairy tales, but the story may have grown from ancient religious beliefs about fire, light, and life. This movement from mythology to folklore happened as myth-tellers stopped believing in the old religion and turned its stories into enjoyable fairy tales.

Children's stories about the terrifying witch Baba Yaga are often called folklore. Yet Baba Yaga may be based on an ancient Slavic goddess of nature.

The western Slavs worshipped a god named Triglav. With his three heads, Triglav watched over three realms: sky, earth, and underworld. Much of what we know about Triglav is thanks to 12th-century Christian monks. The monks wrote about the destruction of the god's temple and statue by churchmen trying to convert the Slavs to Christianity.

Two Pigeons

In the very beginning, there was no sky and no land. There was not even a word that meant "sky" or a word that meant "land." There was only the blue sea, which stretched farther than you can ever imagine. Then, with a swing of his great arm, the god Perun threw his wooden staff. The staff plunged into the very middle of the sea. Quivering and quaking, the staff started to split and to stretch.

Perun's staff stretched into branches and split into twigs. From the twigs sprouted green leaves. For the staff had grown into an oak tree, which towered in the very middle of the sea, its trunk parting the water, its branches reaching to north, south, east, and west.

Sitting upon one of those branches were two pigeons, their feathers bright and their eyes brighter still. One of those pigeons looked north and south, east and west. It preened its pearly feathers as it wondered.

"How shall we create the world?" cooed the first pigeon to the second.

"We shall dive into the sea, down, down, down to the very bottom," cooed the second pigeon to the first. "In our sharp beaks, we will pluck fine sand and pick blue stone. With fine sand and blue stone, we will create the world."

Stretching their wings, craning their necks, the two pigeons plummeted from their branch, cracked the blue mirror of the sea, and swam. Deeper and deeper they paddled, the water surging and rippling around their wings. From the pigeons' beaks, bubbles rose and broke.

At last, on the dark seabed, those two pigeons plucked fine sand and picked blue stone. Heavy with their purpose, the pigeons swam to the water surface. Then they soared, far and wide, as they sowed that fine sand.

From the scattered sand was formed the black earth, green grass, and white ice. Where the pigeons' claws scratched the sand, they made looped rivers and jagged valleys.

Where their feathers ruffled the sand, they made humped hills and cragged mountains.

Then the two pigeons flapped higher and higher, far above Perun's oak tree. Twisting their downy necks, the pigeons hurled blue stones as hard as they could. From those blue stones was formed the blue sky, which was a dome as delicate as the inside of a pigeon's egg.

Again the two pigeons hurled their blue stones, again and again. Perun smiled as each of those spinning stones began to gleam and glow, growing into the sun, the moon, and every one of the shining stars.

Perun Fact Box

MOTHER According to some historians, Perun's mother was Percunatele, a goddess of thunder.

FATHER Unknown

POWERS Perhaps the greatest of the gods, Perun was master of the sky, thunder, lightning, rain, and oak trees. He threw deadly thunderbolts, but his even more dangerous weapons were golden apples, which killed anyone they hit.

Perun Battles Veles

The great god Perun had an enemy named Veles. While Perun was god of the bright sky, Veles was god of the earth and underworld, the dark home of the dead. As long as each god stayed in his own realm, there was order in the world, but one day Veles crept into the heavens ...

Veles liked to take the form of a dragon, with the fur of a bear and the body of a snake. In this shape, Veles wound around the roots of the oak tree that grew at the middle of the world. Yet, one day, Veles decided to slither from his underground caves and to coil up the tree's trunk, into the heavenly realm of Perun. Then Veles opened his mouth wide—and swallowed Perun's wife, who was named Mokosh.

At once, Perun threw thunderbolts at Veles, but fleeing fast from his enemy, Veles transformed himself into trees, people, and galloping animals. At long last, one of Perun's thunderbolts hit Veles, who was killed instantly. The dragon's skin burst, freeing Mokosh and spraying the world in water. Yet Veles did not stay dead for long: Like a snake, he grew a new skin. He curled himself among the roots of the oak and waited for his next chance to coil up the tree's trunk.

OAK TREE

As in Norse mythology, a giant tree grew at the middle of the world. This oak tree supported the sky and, through its trunk and roots, connected the heavens, earth, and underworld. Some tales tell us that the tree grew from Perun's staff. Shrines to Perun were often located underneath ancient oak trees.

VELES

Veles was said to slither up the oak tree once every year, which explained the changing seasons. The dry season came while Veles was in the underworld. This season was followed by thunderstorms during the battle with Perun, then finally by rain.

PERUN

With his fiery thunderbolts, Perun restored order to the world after chaos. While Perun represented air and fire, Veles represented earth and water. It is possible that the ancient Slavs believed the world was made of these four elements, which must be kept in balance.

MOKOSH

A mother goddess, Mokosh watched over women, childbirth, and women's traditional work, such as spinning wool and weaving. Some tales tell us that, after her kidnapping by Veles, Mokosh spent half the year in the underworld and half in the heavens with Perun.

Gods and Goddesses

Some Slavic gods and goddesses were worshipped across the whole region—from modern-day Germany to Russia—where the Slavs lived. Other deities were worshipped only by certain tribes or were given different names by different Slavic peoples.

SVETOVIT

Worshipped in eastern Germany, Svetovit was god of harvest. Statues of the god held a hollow horn and had four heads, which watched over the world in every direction. During the yearly harvest festival, a priest poured alcohol into the statue's horn as he asked Svetovit to watch over the crops for another year.

MORANA

Known by different names across the region, Morana (or Marzanna or Marena) was both the goddess of death and the goddess of the rebirth that follows death, since new growth always follow the frozen darkness of winter. Morana was worshipped at a festival that marked the end of winter and the beginning of spring.

SVAROZHITS

This god of fire was probably worshipped across the whole Slavic region. He was the son of Svarog, a god of the sky, and the brother of Dazhbog. Historians tell us that a wooden temple to Svarozhits stood in the town of Rethra, which lay in the region of today's Germany.

DEVANA

Devana was goddess of the wild, forests, and hunting. Her name and nature were similar to the Roman goddess Diana, who was closely related to the Greek goddess of hunting, named Artemis (see page 16). All these goddesses may have grown from one ancient goddess of Europe or western Asia.

DAZHBOG

Dazhbog was a major god who was worshipped by most Slavic tribes, under names such as Dabog and Dazibogu. He was god of the sun, carrying it through the heavens on its daily travels. Each night, he journeyed through the underworld before reappearing on the eastern horizon.

ZORYA

Goddess of dawn, Zorya was the daughter of Dazhbog. Every morning, she opened the gate to her father's palace so he could set out. According to Russian myths, Zorya had a twin sister, named Zorya Vechernyaya ("evening shining"), who was goddess of dusk.

Dazhbog Fact Box

MOTHER	Unknown
FATHER	Svarog, a god of the sky
POWERS	Dazhbog controlled the sun's life-giving power. His name probably means "giving god" in the ancient Slavic language. According to some myths, he was reborn every morning as a young man, but by sunset he had grown elderly.

The Firebird

An old, white-bearded man rode through the darkening forest. The man was an archer, his bow bouncing on his back as his horse galloped. Through the branches, the archer glimpsed a light ahead. The light brightened, until the archer saw it shone from a feather that lay on the muddy ground. The archer scrambled from his horse to grasp that feather, which glimmered red as flame.

"Do not touch that feather!" cried the archer's horse. "If you do, you will face terrible trials and troubles."

The archer did not listen to his horse's words. Stuffing the feather into his tunic, he galloped to the king's palace. He was certain the king would give him wonderful gifts in return for this feather.

Yet the king was both greedy and cruel. "Bring me the bird that shed this feather! Fetch me the firebird or I will cut off your head!" he shouted at the archer.

Now the archer wept into his horse's mane. "Why did I not listen to your warning?" he cried.

"Fear not," said the horse. "Sprinkle wheat onto the forest floor, then hide among the leaves and branches."

The archer did as he was instructed. Sure enough, there was soon a flicker of flame among the treetops, then the firebird swooped, a bright streak through the branches. The bird landed among the wheat and began to peck. The archer crept close, closer, closer, until he could snatch at the firebird's glowing tail.

The firebird squawked, fluttered, flapped for the freedom of the air—but the archer held it fast by its tail feathers.

Cradling the firebird, the archer galloped to the king. That greedy king was delighted with the shining bird, but he wanted even more. "Since you have been cunning enough to catch the firebird," he told the archer, "now bring me Princess Vasilisa so I can marry her. She lives in the valley beyond the mountains."

The archer rode to that distant valley, where he found the princess upon a lake in a silver boat, rowing with golden oars. "Princess Vasilisa," said the archer, "the king invites you to his palace to see the magical firebird. Will you come with me?"

Princess Vasilisa rode eagerly to the king's palace, with the archer galloping beside her. As soon as the king set eyes on the princess, he asked her to marry him. Yet the princess was not pleased with this offer, for the king's cruelty was known far and wide.

"I will marry you," said Vasilisa to the king, "if you first punish this archer by bathing him in boiling water!"

As the king's servants lit a fire under a cauldron of water, the archer wept into his horse's mane. "Why did I not listen to your warning?" he cried.

"Fear not," said the horse. "I have cast a spell to protect you from the scalding water."

So, as the water began to bubble, the archer stepped into the cauldron. Vasilisa gasped, for she had expected the archer to save himself by galloping into the forest on his trusty horse. She had only hoped for a reason not to marry that greedy king.

Vasilisa wept with joy when the archer stepped from the water. For he was transformed! His white beard was glistening brown! He shone with youth and beauty.

"I want to be young and beautiful, too!" cried the king, leaping into that cauldron of boiling water. The foolish king was dead in a moment.

Now the archer became king of that land. And as the archer walked with Princess Vasilisa, the firebird fluttered into the forest.

Firebird Fact Box

MOTHER	Unknown
FATHER	Unknown
POWERS	After finding one of the firebird's tail feathers, heroes are driven to set out on long and dangerous journeys to capture the bird. The firebird's captor meets with either great good luck or a terrible doom.

Nature Spirits

As well as worshipping many gods and goddesses, the Slavic people worshipped nature spirits. These spirits lived in water, forests, or fields. They could be helpful or harmful to humans.

The ancient Slavs offered prayers and gifts to these nature spirits in the hope of a good harvest, hunt, or fishing trip. Since almost everyone relied on weather, water, and land for survival, nature spirits were of great importance. In fact, in the days before Christianity, these spirits might have been as important as any god or goddess.

After the arrival of Christianity, stories about nature spirits—and belief in them—were kept alive in folklore. The spirits appeared in fairy tales and songs as cruel, mischievous, or kindly creatures. For parents, tales of unkind spirits continued to have an important purpose: They stopped children wandering too far from home. Up to the present day, some hunters, farmers—and those who believe in the old religion—still ask these spirits for success.

RUSALKA

Known by different names across the Slavic region, a *rusalka* was a female water spirit. Today's folklore tells us that *rusalki* are cruel toward humans, yet they may once have been kindly spirits that brought life-giving water to farmers' fields.

VODYANOY

Called a *vodyanoy* in Russian but a *vodník* in Czech, a *vodyanyk* in Ukrainian, a *vodeni mož* in Slovene, and a *topielec* in Polish, this water demon appears in many Slavic fairy tales. When angered, the demon washes away bridges and drowns people and farm animals.

POLEVIK

A *polevik* was a grass- or hay-haired spirit of the fields. According to folklore, farmers must beware angering a *polevik* by falling asleep in the fields. However, a *polevik* can be pleased by giving it gifts of eggs or a rooster.

VILA

A *vila* was a female nature spirit of the air, land, or water. In today's fairy tales, a *vila* may show kindness to humans by giving magical objects or healing wounds. A *vila* may also be cruel by destroying crops or stealing children.

LESHY

This guardian of the forest may once have been the forest god. In today's folklore, Leshy takes the shape of fierce animals to punish humans for disrespecting the forest. His usual appearance has both human and plant-like characteristics, with leafy hair and twiggy fingers.

BABA YAGA

With a name meaning "evil old woman," this forest-living witch appears in many fairy tales, usually as a child-eater. She has a house with chicken legs and flies in a bowl, sweeping away her tracks with a broom. It is likely Baba Yaga once played a part in the Slavic religion, but we cannot know if she was a goddess—perhaps of magic—or an evil demon.

Inuit Mythology

The homeland of Inuit peoples is the Arctic and subarctic regions of Greenland, northern Canada, the US state of Alaska, and northeastern Russia. Inuit lands border the Arctic Ocean, which is largely covered by ice throughout the year. The Inuit religion grew in this harsh climate, where ice and bitter cold prevent farming the land. Fierce storms and dark winter days present more challenges. Traditionally, most Inuit were hunters and fishers, gathering seaweeds and wild plants, such as berries and grasses, when possible.

As is the case with mythologies from around the world, Inuit myths can tell us about the lives of the people who first told them. For example, there is no Inuit goddess of farming, but there is a goddess of hunting, named Pinga, and a goddess of weather, named Qailertetang. The myths can also teach us about the issues that have been important to Inuit peoples over many centuries. For example, we learn from stories about the goddess Sedna and god Nanook that respect for the land, the sea, and their animals is at the heart of Inuit life. Without caring for these precious shared resources—which cannot be taken for granted—disaster awaits. No less important in Inuit stories is respect for other humans, as we learn from "The Seal" on page 56. For hundreds of years, such stories have been told to children to help them learn about their people's values.

Today, many Inuit people follow another religion or none, yet plenty hold the Inuit gods and goddesses, creatures, and spirits close to their hearts. Although the stories told here may be hundreds of years old, they are still alive today—and they still have truths to tell us, not just about Inuit peoples, but about every human's place in our precious, fragile world.

In the past, Inuit peoples hunted polar bears for their meat and warm fur. The god of polar bears, Nanook, took the form of a giant bear. He decided whether a hunter had shown enough respect to be rewarded with success.

Sedna is the Inuit goddess of the sea and of ocean-living animals, which swim among the tendrils of her hair. If Sedna believes that a hunter or fisher deserves and needs food, she chooses which animals to free from her hair.

The Seal

There was once a boy who lived with his grandmother beside the sea. Their hut, made from stones and grass, was very small. Their bowls were very empty, since the boy had no father or grandfather to go hunting. In all the village where the boy and his grandmother lived, only one hunter brought meat to fill their stomachs. That kind hunter's name was Kiviuq.

Every morning when the boy ran outside to play, he dressed in a parka made from the skins of seabirds that his grandmother caught. And every morning, the men of the village laughed at the boy's flimsy clothes. For all those hunters wore the thick, furry skins of the seals they hunted.

"Tweet tweet! Why don't you grow wings and fly away?" laughed the hunters at the boy.

If Kiviuq was close, he stopped the other hunters' unkindness at once: "Leave the boy alone," he cried. "Don't you have anything better to do?"

Yet, when Kiviuq was at sea in his kayak, there was no one to stop the hunters' laughter. No one to stop them pulling and ripping the boy's parka. On those days, the boy ran home with tears on his cheeks. His grandmother muttered angrily as she patched that parka.

Then came the morning that Kiviuq brought grandmother a whole sealskin. "You will know what to do with it, Grandmother," said Kiviuq as he set off for the beach.

"I do know," she answered.

At once, the grandmother set to work, stitching with her bone needle until she had made the boy a suit of new clothes. Yet the grandmother stitched a strange suit. When the boy put it on, only his big black eyes could be seen.

The rest of him was wrapped in sealskin from the top of his head to the tips of his toes.

"Now go to the beach," said the grandmother to the boy, "and leap into the sea."

The boy ran to the beach, darting past the hunters, who were readying their kayaks for a day at sea. On he ran past Kiviuq, who gave a strange smile.

The boy splashed into the waves. Yet as soon as his sealskin feet and fingers touched the water, they became flippers. Whiskers sprouted from his cheeks. So with wiggles of his furry body, flicks of his strong flippers, that seal began to swim out to sea.

"What a beautiful seal!" cried the hunters, leaping into their kayaks. "Let's catch him!"

Kiviuq paddled out to sea with the others, eager to see what the magical seal would do.

On swam the seal, farther and farther from land. As the hunters' arms tired from paddling, their hearts only ached harder to catch that beautiful seal. On, on, on swam the seal until the hunters were so far from land that it was not even a streak on the horizon.

Now a great storm churned the sea. The water surged into towering waves that crashed on the hunters' kayaks, smashing them, tipping them, flooding them. When at last the storm died, there was only one kayak and one hunter on all the blue ocean. And that hunter was kindly Kiviuq, who paddled onward to a new adventure.

The seal swam back to the shore, where he became a boy once more.

Kiviuq Fact Box

MOTHER Unknown

FATHER A half-man, half-seal being known as a Tuutalik

POWERS Also known as Qiviuq, Qooqa, and Qayaq, Kiviuq was a wandering hero with extraordinary strength and bravery. He was also an *angakkuq* (a person with healing powers) who could talk with animals and create fog.

Fierce Spirits

Inuit myths and folklore tell of dangerous spirits and monsters. In the harsh region where these stories were born, these fierce spirits act as important warnings—to children or careless adults—of the dangers of sea ice or hunting alone.

QALLUPILLUK

The Qallupilluk live under the ice that covers the Arctic Ocean. These spirits lie in wait for children who play on the ice, snatching them away to underwater caves. Qallupilluk are a clear warning to children that they must never venture onto the fragile sea ice.

MAHAHA

These creatures lie in wait for lone hunters during the dark winter months. With their long fingers and nails, Mahahas tickle their victims to death. As they kill, they giggle and grin with pleasure.

AMAROK

In the traditional stories of Greenland, this gigantic wolf will follow, kill, and eat a hunter who is foolish enough to hunt alone after sunset. In Alaska, there are similar stories about Amaguq, a shape-shifting trickster spirit that often takes the form of a wolf.

TAQRIAQSUIT

Also known as shadow people, the Taqriaqsuit live all around us, in a world similar to our own but impossible for humans to see. Although the Taqriaqsuit can only be glimpsed by the shadow they cast, their footsteps and laughter can be heard if we listen closely. Sometimes Taqriaqsuit invite humans into their world, but those people never return.

IJIRAAT

These shape-shifting creatures will take the form of any Arctic animal, from a caribou to a fox. Yet, whatever shape they take, an Ijiraat can always be recognized by its glowing red eyes. Some stories tell us that an Ijiraat will steal a child that wanders too far from home.

INUPASUGJUK

Tales from Canada's far north tell us that these giants like to capture humans so they can play with them as if they are dolls. Female Inupasugjuk carry humans in the pouches of their traditional fur jackets, which are known as *amautiit*.

Inupasugjuk Fact Box

CHILDREN Long ago, these giants are said to have had children with humans, creating a group of immensely strong people named the Tuniit. Historians think that stories of the Tuniit were based on a real group of people called the Dorset people, who lived in Arctic North America before the arrival of the Inuit around 1,000 years ago.

POWERS The Inupasugjuk are hardy enough to spend their whole lives on the ice of the Arctic Ocean. They travel south into Inuit lands only in winter, when the ice is thick enough to withstand their immense feet.

Aztec Mythology

The Aztec civilization flourished in Mexico from around 1300 to 1521, when it was conquered by the Spanish. Aztec life was based around great stone cities, the largest of them named Tenochtitlán, in the Valley of Mexico. In the fertile land around their cities, the Aztecs grew crops such as maize (corn), beans, and squashes. Aztec religion grew from the earlier beliefs of people living in the Mexico region, including the Maya and Olmec. For example, the Aztec feathered serpent god named Quetzalcoatl looks like the feathered serpent worshipped by the Olmec, who were powerful from around 1200 BCE to 400 BCE.

The Aztecs built temples at the top of stepped pyramids, which symbolized the mountains that were home to gods. Temples were where priests carried out sacrifices of blood, animals, and humans, since it was believed that creation could continue only if it was fed with life. Priests carefully timed all festivals, sacrifices, and farming activities according to the calendar, which was, in fact, two calendars: a 365-day farming calendar called *xiuhpohualli* (which, like our own calendar, was based on the sun), and a 260-day religious calendar called *tonalpohualli*. The two calendars matched up every 18,980 days, after 52 *xiuhpohualli* years and 73 *tonalpohualli* years.

We know about Aztec religion and myths from Aztec temples, sculptures, and painted books, as well as myths written down after the Spanish conquest. Perhaps the best-known myth tells of the founding of Tenochtitlán (see page 66). Historians believe that the Aztecs founded Tenochtitlán in around 1325, building on an island in shallow Lake Texcoco. The Aztecs then built artificial islands—using wooden stakes, reeds, and piled soil—on which to farm. Today, most of Lake Texcoco has been drained and is occupied by the capital of Mexico: Mexico City. The story of Tenochtitlán's founding is celebrated on the Mexican flag, which shows a golden eagle sitting on a cactus while eating a snake.

In Aztec art, gods and goddesses were shown wearing face and body paint. Each shade of paint had a different meaning, with green-blue—worn here by the rain god Tláloc—representing water and blooming plants. Paint, made from minerals and natural materials such as soot, was also worn by priests, warriors, and people taking part in rituals.

Mictlantecuhtli was god of Mictlan, the underworld of the dead. His wife was Mictecacihuatl, who watched over the festivals of the dead. After blending with Christian traditions brought to Mexico by the Spanish, these festivals evolved into today's Day of the Dead, usually celebrated in early November, when people remember family and friends who have died, wear skull face paint, and eat sugar skulls.

Cipactli the Crocodile

At the very start of the world, there was nothing but water, in which swam an immense crocodile named Cipactli. The crocodile was so hungry and swirled the waters so violently, that nothing else could exist.

Four brother gods decided to take action against Cipactli. They were Tezcatlipoca, black god of the north; Huitzilopochtli, blue god of the south; Xipe Totec, red god of the east; and Quetzalcoatl, white god of the west. To catch Cipactli, Tezcatlipoca stuck out his foot, wiggling his toes to attract the hungry monster.

As the crocodile munched on Tezcatlipoca's foot, the four gods grabbed its scaly, slimy body—and pulled it to the north, south, east, and west, ripping it apart. Working together, the four gods then created the world from Cipactli's body. Its head became the thirteen heavens, its body the earth, and its tail the underworld of the dead. Some say that its four legs became the four water deities Tláloc, Chalchiuhtlicue, Huixtocihuatl, and Chicomecoatl.

TEZCATLIPOCA

God of night and darkness, this god held a mirror made of shiny black stone called obsidian. Such mirrors were used by priests, who gazed into them to guess the future. Tezcatlipoca could take the form of a jaguar, a fierce cat that often hunts at night. When in human form, he painted his skin with yellow and black stripes.

QUETZALCOATL

One of the most important Aztec deities, Quetzalcoatl was god of the wind, light, and life. He also had responsibility for priests, crafts, learning, and calendars. He often took the form of a feathered snake, suggesting his control of the heavens (as a bird) and land (as a snake).

CIPACTLI

Cipactli had the snapping jaws and terrifying strength of a crocodile, but wriggled like a fish and was as slimy as a frog. The monster ate everything it could catch with its many mouths, which sprouted at every joint on its body. After being ripped apart by the four gods, Cipactli remained alive, demanding human blood for its many mouths, as repayment for its sacrifice.

XIPE TOTEC

His face painted with red and yellow stripes, Xipe Totec was god of the seasons, farming, and metalwork. The god removed his own skin, as a snake does, to give food to humankind. This echoes the way that maize seeds crack their outer layer before starting to sprout.

HUITZILOPOCHTLI

Huitzilopochtli was god of fire, war, and sacrifice. He used a fire serpent named Xiuhcoatl as a weapon. He often took the form of a hummingbird, since warriors who died in battle were reincarnated as hummingbirds.

Gods and Goddesses

The Aztecs believed in *teotl*, a sacred power that creates and flows through everything. This force could take the form of the many gods and goddesses worshipped by the Aztecs. The most important of these gods and goddesses controlled the phenomena that were most important to Aztec life: sun and rain, crops and fire, birth and death.

TLÁLOC

Tláloc was god of rain and freshwater springs, the bringer of life-giving water to fields, animals, and humans. The four-fanged, green-painted god was believed to live in the mountain known as Cerro Tláloc, where shrines were built and rituals were held.

TONATIUH

This fierce god carried the fifth sun (the present sun) across the sky each day. It was believed that Tonatiuh could make his daily journey only if he was fed by regular human sacrifices. The high-flying god had eagle's claws and wore their feathers in his headdress.

CHALCHIUHTLICUE

Goddess of childbirth, rivers, lakes, and storms, Chalchiuhtlicue was sister or wife of the rain god Tláloc. While bringing life to crops, she also watched over women and children. Aztec artworks often showed her releasing a stream of water, in which swim a boy baby and girl baby.

CHANTICO

This goddess had responsibility for the fires that burned in the hearths of homes, where the Aztecs cooked and warmed themselves. She also gave courage to warriors and skill to stonecutters.

MAYAHUEL

Mayahuel was goddess of the maguey, a flowering plant with tall, spiky leaves. Threads from maguey plants were used for making cloth and ropes, while the sap was turned into an alcoholic drink named *octli*.

Centeotl Fact Box

MOTHER	Xochiquetzal, goddess of fertility, beauty, and love
FATHER	Piltzintecuhtli, god of the rising sun and healing
POWERS	As guardian of the Aztecs' essential food source, Centeotl was one of the most powerful gods. He is said to have made a dangerous journey to the underworld to fetch other wonderful crops for humans, including cotton and sweet potatoes.

CENTEOTL

His skin painted yellow, this god was lord of maize, also known as corn, which was the Aztecs' most important crop. In Aztec artworks, he was often shown with ears of maize and corn cobs in his headdress.

Founding Tenochtitlán

The Aztecs did not always live in the Valley of Mexico. Long ago, the Aztecs lived in Aztlán, far to the north, beneath a towering cliff of seven caves, beside the Lake of the Moon. In that place, the Aztecs were treated cruelly by their rulers. The Aztecs longed for freedom.

One morning, as he stood beside the Lake of the Moon, an Aztec fisherman heard a tinkling voice. "Go now, go now," trilled the voice.

The man twisted and turned to see who spoke. He could see only a blue hummingbird, its curved beak delving into an orange heliconia flower.

"Did you speak?" asked the fisherman.

Now the hummingbird hovered—its swift wings a blur—in front of the fisherman's startled face. "Go now, go now," peeped the bird again.

The fisherman ran to tell his people's priest, who fell to his knees, for he knew that this hummingbird was none other than Huitzilopochtli, blue god of the south. Then the priest breathed a shivering sigh of joy and fear. "I have long known," cried the priest, "that we must leave here, must find a new land to call our home. Yet, for year upon year, I have waited for a sign that the gods will bless our journey. Now we have it!"

So the Aztecs packed up their pots and hoes, picked up their children, and set out for the south. Day after day they walked, their feet bitten by weeds and rocks, thistles and thorns, vipers and spiders. Week after week they trudged, their backs bent to breaking, until the priest looked around him. They had reached a green valley through which a sparkling river curled. "This would be a fine place to settle," said the priest to his exhausted people.

At once, a blue hummingbird darted from a palicourea bush. It hovered before the priest's wide eyes. "If you listen to my words," chirruped the hummingbird, "your people will build a city, an empire, greater than this land has ever seen. Yet you must not sow your seeds, stretch your roots, unfurl your buds, until you reach a wide lake. There you must watch for a sign. Where an eagle perches

on a cactus, devouring a snake, that is where you must sow." Then the hummingbird flitted into the scrub.

So the Aztecs hiked on, for month after month, some say for year after year. At last, they found themselves on the shore of a wide lake, shallow and swampy, its reeds busy with scarlet dragonflies.

"Look! There!" cried a little girl, pointing to a low island that peeked above the lake's blue water.

There, on a nopal cactus, was an eagle, its feathers glinting gold. In the eagle's hooked beak wriggled a rattlesnake.

The priest was wise enough to know the meaning of this sign: There, on that island, the Aztecs would rise like eagles, holding power over plants and beasts, their fame undimmed by death.

So the Aztecs built a city on the island, turning its green grass to golden stone. They called the city Tenochtitlán, which meant "place of the cactus stones." Using sticks and soil, they built gardens on the lake, turning its blue water to green fields. And their bright city's fame lived on and on, despite disaster, disease, and even death.

Huitzilopochtli Fact Box

MOTHER	Omecihuatl, the first goddess
FATHER	Ometecuhtli, the first god
POWERS	His name meaning "hummingbird of the south," Huitzilopochtli was patron god of the Aztecs' capital, Tenochtitlán. Hummingbirds were important to the Aztecs because they slow their body processes during the dry season, appearing to die, then revive at the start of the rainy season, appearing to be reborn. Like a hummingbird, bright Huitzilopochtli held power over death and darkness.

Egyptian Mythology

From around 3100 BCE, the ancient Egyptian civilization thrived around North Africa's River Nile. Under the rule of pharaohs (who were kings or, occasionally, queens), the ancient Egyptians mastered irrigation (using canals and simple machines to carry the Nile's water to fields), mummification (treating and wrapping dead bodies so they did not decay), writing (using symbols called hieroglyphs), and ambitious building projects. These projects included stone temples for worshipping gods and goddesses, as well as—from around 2700 to 1500 BCE—pyramids that served as tombs for pharaohs. By 30 BCE, when Egypt came under Roman control, the ancient civilization's most glorious days had ended.

More than 1,500 Egyptian gods and goddesses have been counted. While some were important throughout Egypt, others were worshipped in one town or had a minor role, such as being god of a particular day of the month. Some foreign gods—from nearby Nubia and Canaan—were adopted during Egypt's long history, while dead pharaohs also joined the ranks of the gods. Over time, gods and goddesses changed and developed, taking new characteristics and roles, growing or shrinking in importance. For example, the king of the gods, Amun, was fused with the sun god Ra, becoming all-powerful Amun-Ra from around 1600 BCE.

Egyptian myths have reached us thanks to ancient writings such as funeral texts. Created to help the newly dead in the underworld, these were collections of stories, pictures, and magic spells that were written on papyrus rolls, mummy bandages, coffins, and tomb walls. Most myths are about the constant battle between order (*maat*) and chaos (*isfet*). The creation myths explain how the gods first created order from chaos. Other myths explain how natural, endlessly repeated cycles—such as the sun god Ra's daily journey across the sky or the yearly Nile floods—continue to impose order, over and over again.

At first, Amun was a fertility god who was worshipped only in the city of Thebes. After Thebes became Egypt's capital, Amun grew in importance, with his temple complex at Karnak one of the largest—covering 250,000 sq m (2.7 million sq ft)—in Egypt. Amun's skin was often shown as blue, which represented the fertility of the River Nile.

Seshat was goddess of knowledge, writing, mathematics, astronomy, and architecture. She was often pictured holding a knotted rope, which was used to measure the foundations for buildings. She wore a cheetah- or leopard-skin dress, its pattern representing the stars. Above her head was a hieroglyph that named her.

Creating the World

At first, there was only the god Nun. That god was a vast ocean of churning chaos, which filled all the universe. Then a pyramid-shaped mound pushed up through the swirling water. On the mound's summit sprouted a lotus flower—and from that flower was born Ra, god of the sun.

As the sun rose for the first time, Ra decided to create order from the chaos. He pushed aside Nun, then made other gods and goddesses to help him. He made Geb, god of the earth, who laid himself flat. Arching over Geb, Ra placed Nut, goddess of the sky. Beneath Nut, his arms supporting her, was Shu, god of the air.

Yet, as Ra worked, another being was born from Nun's waters. This was Apep, the snake of darkness and disorder. He curled himself beneath Geb, in the underworld, where he could wait for a chance to destroy Ra's creation. Perhaps, one day, Apep will get his way—and chaos will return.

NUT

The ancient Egyptians often depicted the sky goddess as a star-covered woman who arched over the earth. Nut and her brother Geb are unusual in world mythologies, which usually have a male sky deity and female earth deity.

APEP

This dark god was the greatest enemy of shining Ra. Every day he waited for sunset, when Ra must enter the underworld in his journey around the world. Through the night, the two gods battled, with Ra always victorious at sunrise.

NUN

God of chaos, Nun was the first deity. Nun made—and is—a vast ocean, which surrounds the bubble of sky, air, and earth formed by the other gods. Some believe that, one day, Nun's ocean will once again be all that exists.

RA

God of the sun, order, and pharaohs, Ra ruled over all creation. He carried the sun across the daytime sky in a small boat called a barque. He was often depicted with the head of a falcon, on which rests the sun. The high-flying falcon symbolized Ra's daily journey.

SHU

God of the air and wind, Shu was seen as a calming influence, so he was also god of peace. He was often depicted wearing an ostrich feather, which was a symbol of lightness. When forced to defend Ra from the forces of chaos, he became fiercer, taking a lion's head.

GEB

As god of the earth, Geb made crops grow, while his laughter made earthquakes. Like many other gods and pharaohs, he was often depicted wearing a false beard, which was attached by a long thread. This was a sign of the gods and pharaohs' difference from ordinary men.

Tefnut's Anger

Tefnut was born from a gob of spit. The sun god Ra spat into the desert, then from that puddle grew Tefnut, goddess of rain, mist, and dew. Tefnut was a generous goddess, giving water to the River Nile and life to the crops. Yet Tefnut had a terrifying temper. And when she was angry, she took the form of a lion.

Tefnut had served Ra for many years, by swiping her claws at any snake or scorpion that dared to stop his daily journey around the earth. So you can imagine Tefnut's anger when the sun god asked her sister, Bastet, to protect him instead.

"Bastet, goddess of cats, I need your swift jaws to save me from that wriggling serpent Apep," said Ra, never sparing a thought for Tefnut.

Seething with fury, Tefnut gave a roar that scattered sparrows into the startled sky. Shu, Tefnut's brother and husband, rushed to her side. Shu was the gentle god of the air. Yet not even Shu's soft, fluttering words could calm Tefnut's rage.

Tefnut's fury had soon turned her brown skin to golden fur, her fingers to glinting claws. In the form of a lion, she bounded from Egypt, across the hot sand, into Nubia. There she found a family of lions to hunt with. Her teeth bloody, she turned her back on Egypt.

With Tefnut far away, no rain fell on Egypt. Only the sun's heavy heat landed on the earth. It frazzled the crops, dried the canals and streams. Soon the animals were thirsty. Children cried for water. Then, as the grain stores emptied, as the animals staggered, children cried for food.

Ra was worried. Not only were his people in danger, but they hid from him, cowering beneath the date palms to escape his baking heat. The people of Egypt offered Ra fewer prayers with every dreadful day that passed. The sun god knew he must act.

"Thoth," called Ra to the wise god of the moon. "Bring Tefnut home."

Thoth took the form of a baboon, then scampered into Nubia. He spoke soothingly to Tefnut: "Most adored goddess, most noble goddess," he said as he scratched at his bristly fur. "Ra is sorry for forgetting your loyalty, your untiring service."

"Tell me more," purred Tefnut.

As the moon god spoke more silvery words, he watched Tefnut's flicking tail grow still. He watched her shed the golden fur from her paws, watched her stretch once again the long brown limbs of a goddess. At last, Thoth watched as Tefnut lost her tufted ears and twitching whiskers.

So Tefnut returned to Egypt, spreading dark clouds across the sapphire sky. Rain spattered onto the parched earth, soaking the soil, bathing the seeds into life. The rain fell

faster and faster, swelling the thirsty Nile, until the river surged over its banks, covering the fields with rich soil, rushing into canals and reservoirs.

As the people of Egypt danced in that wonderful rain, Ra called Tefnut to his side. "You will always be my guardian, my feared, my fierce, my furry Tefnut," he promised.

Yet you can be sure that some thoughtless god or goddess will make Tefnut roar with rage again. Then we will have to wait while that sharp-clawed goddess thrashes her tail. But, do not fear, Tefnut will calm herself—and she will send rain to wash the dusty ground once more.

Tefnut Fact Box

PARENT	Ra, god of the sun and pharaohs
POWERS	Tefnut brought rain, clouds, and moist air, yet—when angry—she brought the opposite: drought, baking heat, and thirst. When in the form of a lion, she was a fierce protector of her father.

Animal Forms

The ancient Egyptians often depicted their gods and goddesses with animal heads or in the form of animals. They believed that their deities could take the shape of animals that matched their nature, whether that was the fierceness of a cobra or the calm of an ibis.

ANUBIS

God of mummification, funerals, and graves, Anubis guided the dead into the underworld. He had the head of a jackal, because that member of the dog family was often seen in cemeteries. Despite his link with death, Anubis held a farming tool called a flail, representing the fertility of the land, and a hieroglyph called *ankh* (a cross with a handle), which meant "life."

WADJET

The goddess Wadjet was protector of Lower Egypt, the kingdom's northern half. She often took the form of a winged Egyptian cobra, a deadly snake. When unified with her sister Nekhbet, the protector of Upper Egypt, she became the guardian of all Egypt.

TAWERET

This goddess watched over pregnancy, birth, and babies. She took the form of a female hippo, since these mammals fiercely protect their young. Children and pregnant women wore amulets showing the goddess with a lion's paws and a crocodile-tail mane, so her frightening appearance would drive away evil spirits. Taweret often held the hieroglyph *sa*, which meant "protection."

THOTH

As god of the moon, time, seasons, and the calendar, Thoth often wore a headdress of the full moon resting on a crescent moon. He was depicted with the head of an ibis, since the bird's curving beak resembled the new moon.

SOBEK

Sobek was god of Nile crocodiles, which are aggressive reptiles—up to 6 m (20 ft) long—that prey on any animal they find. Sobek was linked with the Nile's life-giving water, with the power of pharaohs, and with armies. Egyptians often prayed for his fierce protection.

HATHOR

Hathor was both a goddess of motherhood and one of Egypt's goddesses of the sky. Her role as a mother was often symbolized by having the head of a milk-giving cow. As goddess of the sky, she held a sun disk between her horns. She was worshipped as the mother of pharaohs.

Hathor Fact Box

PARENT	Ra, god of the sun and pharaohs
POWER	Known as the Eye of Ra, Hathor could wield a violent, destructive force that she used to defend the sun god. Hathor was both the daughter and mother of Ra, in a constant cycle of death and rebirth: At sunset, the god of the sun was absorbed into her body, which he had created; at sunrise, she gave birth to him.

The Death of Osiris

Before the pharaohs, Egypt was ruled by the god Osiris. He ruled with great wisdom and justice. Yet Osiris had a brother named Set. Where Osiris loved order, Set loved only chaos. Where Osiris loved peace, Set loved only destruction. And so Set killed Osiris, cut his body into pieces, and scattered those pieces over Egypt. Set seized the throne.

All would have been lost, but Osiris had a wife named Isis. That goddess took the form of a falcon and flew over Egypt on her wide wings. As she soared, she gave high cries of grief, which falcons have been making ever since. Yet Isis's sharp eyes never failed to spy the pieces of her husband's body. She grasped them in her beak.

When Isis had collected every portion of Osiris, she called upon the god Anubis. "Help me make my husband whole," she cried.

Skillful Anubis sewed, washed, and emptied Osiris's body. He dried it with a salt called natron. He perfumed it with cinnamon and cumin. He placed Osiris's lungs, liver, intestines, and stomach in jars. Then Anubis wrapped Osiris's body in fine linen bandages. This was how Osiris became the first mummy. Now his body would never change, never decay.

Isis fanned Osiris's body with her falcon wings, wafting the breath of life into his nostrils. Osiris opened his brown eyes, Isis's feathers brushed his cheek, and—in that bright moment—their son sprang from Isis's body. That son, a baby with gripping fists and kicking toes, was named Horus.

Yet bandage-wrapped Osiris could not remain in the sunlight for long. Now his home must be the underworld. So, from that day forward, wise Osiris ruled over the dead, who found peace in his shady caves. He ensured that each dead soul received its just rewards for a life lived well.

Set continued to rule cruelly over Egypt, sitting proudly on his glistening throne as the people suffered. But, protected by Isis's wings, young Horus was growing in height and strength every day. Like his mother, he could soon take the form of a far-seeing, fast-flying falcon.

When Horus's wings were wider than a fig tree, he knew the time had come to restore order to the world. He flapped fast at Set, knocking him from the throne. The two gods struggled and rolled and grappled. Set's vicious nails ripped out Horus's left eye, yet the brave young god fought on. Finally, with a kick to Set's belly, Horus hurled his uncle into the barren desert lands far from the Nile.

Horus picked up his left eye and sent it into the underworld as a funeral offering for his father. Then, his mother by his side, Horus sat on the throne of Egypt. "Now," said Horus, "the dead and the living know the truth. After every cruel ruler, there will be a wise ruler, after chaos will be order, after death will be rebirth."

Osiris Fact Box

MOTHER	Nut, goddess of the sky
FATHER	Geb, god of the earth
POWERS	Osiris was god of death, yet he offered souls a new, everlasting life in his underworld. His green skin symbolized rebirth, as new green plants reach through the soil after winter or drought.

Yoruba Mythology

The traditional Yoruba religion, called Isese in the Yoruba language, grew among the Yoruba people, who live mainly in Nigeria, Togo, and Benin in West Africa. At the religion's heart is belief in a supreme god, named Olodumare or Olorun. This being is all-powerful, the creator of all things. Olodumare is not worshipped directly, but can be worshipped through spirits named *orishas*. *Orisha* means "selected head." These spirits are godly beings that hold aspects of the supreme god's power. For example, one *orisha* holds the power of the wind, while another *orisha* helps the harvest.

Opposing the *orishas* are the *ajogun*, which means "that which feeds on trouble." While the *orishas* are usually kind to humans, the *ajogun* are at war with humanity. They carry the negative and destructive forces of nature. There are nine major *ajogun*: Iku (death), Arun (disease), Edi (chaos), Egba (laziness), Epe (curses), Ese (affliction), Ewon (imprisonment), Ofo (loss), and Oran (trouble). Yoruba people do not worship the *ajogun*, but they accept them as part of the necessary balance in creation.

Today, the majority of Yoruba people are believers in Islam or Christianity, but the traditional Yoruba religion is still part of many lives. Whatever their religious beliefs, many Yoruba people take part in festivals of the *orishas*, enjoying these opportunities to celebrate their shared traditions. The Yoruba religion also continues to have influence far from West Africa. From the 16th to 19th centuries, more than a million Yoruba men, women, and children were enslaved, then taken aboard ships to the Americas and Caribbean. They carried their beliefs with them. In the New World, traditional Yoruba religion blended with Christianity and other African religions, becoming today's Candomblé religion of Brazil, the Santería religion of Cuba, and the Orisha religion of Trinidad and Tobago.

One of the most important *orishas* is Osun, who holds the powers of love, beauty, and water. She is celebrated at a two-week festival that is held on the banks of the River Osun.

Osanyin is the *orisha* of herbal medicine, which was the only type of medication—in Africa and beyond—until modern times. The *orisha* knows and teaches the valuable properties of leaves and roots. He is often depicted with birds, which carry messages between *orishas* and humans.

Obatala's Work

Creation began with Olodumare, because Olodumare is creation. First, he had the idea of the world. Then he made an ocean, which stretched from far to wide. Everything else was sky. Next, Olodumare created seventeen *orishas*. Sixteen of those *orishas* were male, including Obatala, who had quick hands, and Orunmila, who had quick thoughts. The seventeenth *orisha* was a woman named Osun, who held the power of water.

Olodumare called to his *orishas* from far away: "Make the land and people to live on it."

At once, the *orishas* crowded together, chattering of plans and possibilities. But wise Orunmila's voice rose above the rest. "We need a strong bag, a long gold chain, an empty snail shell, a pile of brown earth, a white chicken, and a palm nut," he cried. "Then Obatala must get to work, for his hands are cleverest."

Obatala listened carefully to Orunmila's instructions, then collected his tools. He packed the earth into the snail shell. He put the shell and palm nut into the bag. The chicken leaped onto his shoulder, where it began to peck at his eyebrows.

As Obatala's fifteen brothers and one sister held tight to one end of the gold chain, he threw the other end over the edge of the sky. The chain dangled down, down, almost as far as the blue ocean below.

Gripping with sweaty hands, squeezing with quivering knees, the chicken pecking his face and the bag rubbing his back, Obatala lowered himself down the chain. Down he slid, until he could see the white crests of waves below. Now he reached into his bag and took out the snail shell. Obatala tipped the brown earth over the ocean. Where once there was nothing but blue water, now there was flat brown land.

"Off you go, little chicken," said Obatala to the bird, which fluttered down to the land.

Just as chickens do today, the bird scratched and kicked, sending up plumes of earth with its claws. Again kicked the chicken, and again, forming high mountains where the earth piled, jagged valleys where its feet gouged.

Now Obatala jumped onto the land he had made. He dug a hole with his strong fingers, then planted the palm nut. At once, the seed sprouted, stretching roots into the earth, reaching a trunk high into the sky. Among the tree's spreading leaves grew nuts. The nuts fell, took root, and stretched into trees. Before Obatala had done more than wipe the sweat from his brow, a forest cloaked the land.

Now came the hardest part of Obatala's work. He called up to Osun: "Sister, soak the earth with wonderful water!" At once, raindrops drenched the soil, making puddles of sodden, sticky clay. Obatala squeezed and stretched and pulled and pressed that clay. One after another, Obatala shaped humans from the clay. His humans were tall, short, long-armed, or big-eared. Each one was different, but Obatala knew each was perfect.

Yet Obatala had only made human forms, as empty of life as his snail shell. It was Olodumare, and Olodumare only, who could give life to those forms. So when Obatala had finished his clay humans, he sat on his heels and waited.

The *orisha* did not have to wait long. A wind ruffled the leaves of the forest, blew gently in the faces of the clay people. Those first humans blinked, quivered, and breathed. Far above him, Obatala heard the *orishas* cheer.

Proud of his day's work, Obatala climbed up the gold chain, helped by the hauling of his brothers and sister. Then, long into the night, the seventeen *orishas* danced to the beat of their *dundun* drums, the shaking of their *sekeres*, and the soaring strings of their *gojes*.

Obatala Fact Box

PARENTS Olodumare, the supreme god

POWERS Obatala was given the power of creation, although life-force—which flows through all things—can only be the gift of his father. Since Obatala created each human with differences, and loved each human equally, he is the protector of people with disabilities.

Orishas

A story tells us that, long ago, the creator Olodumare threw his powers into the air. The spirits who caught the powers became responsible for them. These power-wielding spirits are known as *orishas*. Some Yoruba people say that there are "400 plus 1" *orishas*, while others say there are as many as you can imagine, plus 1.

OKO

An *orisha* of farming, Oko is thanked during the harvest of the white African yam, which is a major crop in West Africa. The *orisha*'s messengers are bees. These insects are important crop pollinators, carrying pollen from male to female flowers.

ESHU

Sometimes depicted with two faces, this *orisha* acts as a messenger between the *orishas* and humans and between the *orishas* and *ajogun*. He also creates balance between opposing forces, such as joy and sorrow, good and bad, just and unjust.

OGUN

Ogun is *orisha* of metalwork and technology. In the past, he was also *orisha* of metal weapons and the warriors who held them. Taxi-, bus-, and truck-drivers may carry an amulet of Ogun to ward off accidents.

OYA

This *orisha* has power over wind and storms. Her violent rainstorms are said to be the source of the River Niger, which is called the Odò-Oya in the Yoruba language. Oya can take the form of an African buffalo. This strong animal is an important grazer in West Africa, maintaining the grassland so that other species can thrive.

OBA

The wife of Shango, Oba is *orisha* of the River Oba, which flows into the River Osun. A story tells us that the *orisha* Osun (see page 78) tricked Oba into cutting off her ear, then feeding it to Shango. Shango was horrified. Ever since, the meeting point of the Rivers Osun and Oba has been dangerously turbulent.

SHANGO

Shango is *orisha* of lightning, thunder, and fire. He wields a double-headed axe, which he uses against the enemies of justice. His necklaces are strung with red and white beads, in groups of four or six, which are his sacred numbers.

Shango Fact Box

MOTHER	Yemonja, an *orisha* of water and motherhood
FATHER	Possibly Aganju, a human king who became an *orisha*
POWERS	One of the most powerful *orishas*, Shango can throw "thunderstones" at those who are unjust, creating lightning and booming thunder. He is able to breathe out fire and smoke through his nostrils.

Chinese Mythology

Over thousands of years, Chinese myths grew among the people of China and nearby lands. These stories form part of Chinese folk religion, which developed in ancient times and continues to have many believers today. At the heart of this religion is the worship of gods, goddesses, and spirits, who may be gods of nature, places, or activities. Some are ancestors (people who lived before) who have become gods due to their good deeds. Many myths are about the gods and goddesses' creation of the world and their teaching of humans.

Chinese myths were influenced by Taoism. This is both a philosophy (a system of ideas for understanding the universe) and a religion, which worships many gods of Chinese folk religion. Taoism took shape in China between 450 and 300 BCE, when its ideas were written in texts such as the *Tao Te Ching*. Taoism itself was influenced by Buddhism (an Indian religion based on leading a pure, good life) and Confucianism (a Chinese philosophy based on respect and kindness). Put simply, Taoism teaches that all things are connected, so humans should try to live in harmony with nature and each other. All things must find a balance of opposing forces: *yin* and *yang*, which are dark and light, earth and fire, inaction and action, female and male. Chinese myths often tell us of beings—such as the great goddess Nüwa (see page 89)—who work to find this balance.

Some Chinese myths can be seen as records of long-ago events, which were passed down as stories from person to person. For example, a myth tells us that the dragon Yinglong (see page 92) showed King Yu where to dig ditches and banks to stop the flooding of his kingdom. This story may be based on Chinese rulers who, from at least 2,300 years ago, worked to control the flooding of the Yellow River. King Yu was held as an example of Taoist action. He also came to be worshipped as a god in Taoism and Chinese folk religion.

A *fenghuang* is a mythical creature that combines *yin* and *yang*, since it is both female and male. Each part of its body represents a Taoist principle: Its head represents goodness, its wing duty, its back decency, its abdomen trustworthiness, and its chest mercy.

The Chinese moon goddess is Chang'e, who lives on the moon with her pet, Yutu ("Jade Rabbit"), for company. This myth grew from the rabbit-shaped dark markings seen on the moon. In 2013, a Chinese robotic spacecraft named *Chang'e 3* landed on the moon, then released a rover named *Yutu* to explore the surface.

Pangu

This is the story of the universe, which we could also call the story of how one thing became two things, then ten thousand things. Let's begin with *wuji*. Before there was anything, there was *wuji*. *Wuji* was featureless and formless. It had no limits, no edges. In *wuji*, all was mixed and mingling. There was not yet *yin* or *yang*, darkness or light, space or matter, reaction or action. Something had to happen.

What happened was an egg. This was the first thing that existed. The egg was born when *yin* separated from *yang*, each pulling itself into being. Now dark balanced light, space balanced matter, reaction balanced action. Each opposite pressed against the other, perfectly weighted. This balance, contained within an egg, was called *taiji*. The egg held the possibility of all things.

For eighteen thousand years, the egg was all that there was. Yet, inside the egg, something was growing. At last, the egg cracked. Out sprang a giant named Pangu. He held an axe.

Pangu was the hairiest giant you can imagine. Thick, silky, soft fur covered him from head to toe. Only his fierce face could be seen among his hair, as well as the horns that sprouted from the top of his head.

To create the world, Pangu knew that he must split *yin* from *yang*. He took his axe and—with a roar as loud as thunder—carved dark from light. Down fell murky, heavy *yin*. It formed the rocky earth. Up sprang light, bright *yang*. It formed the sky. Now there were two things.

Yet Pangu knew that, to make space for all creation, he must keep sky apart from earth. He dropped his axe, then wedged himself between sky and earth, pressing on the sky with his upstretched arms, bracing his broad, furry feet against the earth.

Days passed, then more days. With each day, Pangu grew ten *chi* taller, which lifted the sky ten *chi* higher. At the same time, the earth grew ten *chi* thicker with every day. This continued for another eighteen thousand years.

Pangu Fact Box

PARENTS None

POWERS Pangu held the essential knowledge of *yin* and *yang*. He knew how to separate *yin* from *yang*, yet to hold them in balance, so that the universe can be in harmony. His name means "ancient basin," suggesting that he is the source of all things.

Then, quite suddenly, Pangu died. But from this death came life, because Pangu's body became every one of the ten thousand things that exist.

Pangu's head became the mountains, which continued his work of holding up the sky. His blood flowed as rivers, while his muscles churned into soil. His thick fur became the forests that cloak the land.

Deep inside Pangu, his bones became iron and copper, while his bone marrow twinkled into glittering jewels.

Pangu's last breath became the wind, the mist, and the scudding clouds. His sweat fell as the rain that quenches the land's thirst. Pangu's voice became rumbling thunder. His right eye became the silvery moon, while his left eye spun away from earth, becoming the glowing sun.

Now there was rustling and fluttering in the forests. For Pangu's thick fur had been infested with hopping, biting fleas. Those fleas became all the animals that we know, from stalking tigers to snakes, gentle pandas to cranes. Now there were ten thousand things.

Gods and Goddesses

Hundreds of gods and goddesses appear in Chinese myths. While some of these immortal beings were present from the moment of creation, others were born human, then were deified (turned into gods) for their good deeds.

JADE EMPEROR

Known as Yudi in Chinese, this supreme god rules over the other gods in heaven. He is often depicted on a throne, wearing a robe embroidered with dragons (the symbol of emperors) and holding a tablet of jade, which is carved with orders and laws. Due to its hardness and beauty, the mineral jade is a symbol of heaven and immortal life.

XIHE

A goddess of the sun, Xihe is the mother of ten sun-crows, each of these glowing birds having three legs. The sun-crows live in a mulberry tree in the eastern sea. Every morning, one of the sun-crows takes its turn to ride in its mother's carriage, as she drives from east to west across the sky.

MAZU

Mazu is a sea goddess who takes care of sailors and fishers. It is believed that Mazu once had human form: She was a priestess named Lin Moniang, who may have lived on the southern coast of China in the 10th century. A story tells us that she saved her family when they were caught at sea during a typhoon.

CAISHEN

God of wealth, Caishen holds a rod that turns iron into gold. He rides a black tiger that wards off bad luck. During Chinese New Year celebrations—when people greet each other "*Gong xi fa cai*," which means "Wishing you wealth"—incense is burned in his temple. Before becoming a god, Caishen may have been a holy man named Zhao Gongming.

SHENSHU AND YULÜ

This pair of gods watches over doors and gateways, preventing evil spirits from entering. According to myth, the gods tie bad spirits in ropes, then feed them to tigers.

NÜWA

A mother goddess, Nüwa was creator of humankind. She shaped humans from yellow clay. Nüwa and her brother, Fuxi—who helped her put people in the world—have the faces of humans and the bodies of snakes.

Nüwa Fact Box

MOTHER	Huaxu, an earth goddess, who became pregnant after stepping in Leigong's footprint
FATHER	Leigong, god of thunder
POWERS	A champion of humankind, Nüwa not only created humans but saved them from disaster by mending the sky after it was smashed (see Ao on page 92). Mothers often pray to Nüwa when they need help or advice.

Land of Myth

In Chinese mythology, China is called the "Middle Kingdom," since it was believed to lie at the heart of the universe. The Middle Kingdom described in myths is not identical to the China we know: It is the site of places both real and legendary. This illustration shows the Middle Kingdom's western region.

Geographically, China is bounded by seas to its east, southeast, and south, but the Middle Kingdom is enclosed by Four Seas: the East, South, West, and North. Within these mythical borders, the Middle Kingdom is also surrounded by eight holy mountains, which help to support the weight of heaven.

These holy mountains are studded with caves or hollows known as grotto-heavens. Hidden behind bright clouds and peach trees, grotto-heavens are home to immortal beings. Flowing from holy mountains are strange rivers with bright water. This water gives life to legendary plants such as yao grass, which has yellow flowers that can be made into a love potion.

WEST SEA

Each of the Four Seas is home to a rain dragon. The West Sea, often linked with the real location of Qinghai Lake in central China, is home to a dragon named Ao Run.

MOUNT KUNLUN

The mythical Mount Kunlun has cliffs of jade. Its slopes are dotted with grotto-heavens, where spirits such as Yu Shi, god of rain, can be found. Kunlun not only supports heaven but stretches into it. The palace on Kunlun's summit is home to a mother goddess called the Queen Mother of the West.

WEAK RIVER

Along with the Moving Sands, this river forms a barrier so that unworthy humans cannot reach Mount Kunlun's holy slopes. The river gained its name (Ruoshui in Chinese, which means "weak water") because not even a feather can float in it, preventing anyone from crossing.

LANGGAN TREES

On the slopes of Kunlun are *langgan* trees, which bear blue, red, and green jewels instead of fruit. These jewels are said to give immortality.

MOVING SANDS

The Moving Sands is a dangerous region of fast-drifting sand dunes. The sands are home to a man-eating ogre named Sha Wujing, who has a red beard, blue skin, and a necklace of skulls.

RED RIVER

Along with the white, black, and yellow rivers, the Red River flows from Mount Kunlun. The 3rd-century BCE poet Qu Yuan—who became a water god after his death—wrote that he crossed the river when dragons made a bridge with their long, scaly bodies.

Powerful Creatures

Chinese myths tell of legendary creatures that have the power to do great harm or immense good. Among the most powerful are dragons, which have long, snake-like bodies. Unlike the fearsome dragons and serpents of European mythologies, Chinese dragons usually bring good things.

YINGLONG

This winged dragon's name means "responding dragon." He is a bringer of rain. During droughts in ancient China, people made images of Yinglong in the hope that he would send showers. He showed the legendary King Yu where to dig ditches and banks to stop flooding.

FENGHUANG

Born inside the sun, the *fenghuang* is an immortal bird with an exceptionally beautiful song. It is both male and female at once, with feathers in the Chinese world's five fundamental shades: black, white, red, green, and yellow. Seeing a *fenghuang* is said to bring happiness and peace.

AO

This giant sea turtle saved the world after two battling gods broke the pillars that held up heaven. With Ao's permission, the goddess Nüwa chopped off his legs and used them as new pillars. However, the unequal lengths of Ao's legs make the sky tilt, which is why the sun—viewed from China—does not rise exactly in the east.

ZHULONG

His name meaning "torch dragon," Zhulong is a god of the sun. By opening his eyes, he creates daylight. By closing them, he brings night. The wind and rain are said to come at his call.

PIXIU

A *pixiu* is a winged creature, part-lion and part-dragon, that protects the souls of the dead, as well as drawing wealth toward the living. A *pixiu*'s fangs are used to attack evil spirits, draining their life-essence and converting it to wealth. A female *pixiu* has two antlers, while a male has one.

XIANGLIU

A snake with nine human heads, Xiangliu destroyed the land wherever he went, bringing disaster to humans. Luckily for humankind, Xiangliu was killed by the goddess Nüwa.

Xiangliu Fact Box

MOTHER	Unknown
FATHER	Possibly Gonggong, a destructive water god
POWERS	Xiangliu wrought havoc in any ecosystem: All the land he breathed on was soon covered in a flood of poisonous water. His nine heads gobbled up every plant and animal they saw.

The Great Race

Jade Emperor noticed that humans found it difficult to keep track of the passing of time, as days became months and harvest turned to winter then spring. He decided to give humans a wonderful gift: the calendar. Jade Emperor called thirteen animals to his palace: cat, dog, dragon, goat, horse, monkey, ox, pig, rabbit, rat, rooster, snake, and tiger.

"Welcome, animals," said Jade Emperor, as dog sniffed rat, who nibbled horse's tail. "You thirteen animals will take part in a race. The years on my calendar will be named after each animal in the order that you finish the race."

"Mmmeow," purred cat, "mmmarvelous."

"Off you go," said Jade Emperor. "The finish line is down the mountain, on the other side of the Yellow River. Beware the water, which is dangerously fast flowing."

Off raced the animals, while Jade Emperor positioned himself on the opposite bank of the Yellow River, in the shade of a peach tree. Before long, he saw rat scurrying toward him. Close behind rat was the sturdy, broad-shouldered ox.

"You are the winner, rat," said Jade Emperor. "But how did such a small creature cross the river first?"

"Kind ox let me ride on his shoulders while he waded across," chirped rat. "Cat jumped onto ox, too, but I shoved cat into the water. She floated downstream, so we won't be seeing puss for a while. Then, as ox scrambled up the riverbank, I scampered ahead of him."

At that moment, tiger sprang to Jade Emperor's feet. With her furry paw, she cleaned the water from her ears. "Although I am strong," explained tiger, "the current pushed me downstream, so I could not keep up with ox."

Now rabbit bounced toward Jade Emperor. "I'm fourth, I'm fourth," she squeaked. "I hopped from stone to stone across the river. It was a winding journey, but at last I leaped onto a piece of driftwood that washed me ashore."

Raising a wind that ruffled Jade Emperor's robe, dragon swooped through the air, landing beside the peach tree. "Beautiful dragon," said Jade Emperor, "why did you not arrive first, since you could fly across the river?"

"I soared over a village where people cried out for rain," answered dragon. "I puffed until the clouds broke, filling those thirsty people's buckets and ponds."

At the sound of hooves, the animals turned to see horse approaching. But—as horse galloped toward Jade Emperor—snake slithered from her hoof. Horse slid to a stop, quivering with shock, as snake wriggled to Jade Emperor. "I'm sssssixth," hissed snake, "and horse is sssssseventh."

Goat, monkey, and rooster arrived almost at once, with goat perhaps a little ahead and rooster a little behind. "I found a raft," crowed rooster. "Monkey and goat had the strength to pull it down the bank. Working together, we paddled across the river."

Announcing his arrival with a drenching shake of his wet fur, dog dropped a stick at Jade Emperor's feet. "What took you so long?" asked Jade Emperor. "You can swim and run fast!"

"I've been playing with this stick," woofed dog happily. "And splashing in the water!"

Now only one animal was missing. The sun had set behind Mount Kunlun before pig ambled toward Jade Emperor. "Sorry to keep you waiting," oinked pig. "I felt hungry during the race, so I snuffled for a juicy truffle, then I must have dozed off."

"Never mind, pig," said Jade Emperor. "You are the twelfth and last animal, since cat is nowhere to be seen. Every twelfth year will be called the Year of the Pig. After that, it will be rat's turn again, followed by ox, and so on. Since humans love animals, they will never again forget which year is which!"

Year of the Rat Fact Box

LAST	January 2020–February 2021
NEXT	February 2032–January 2033
POWERS	The winner of the Great Race, rat is the first animal in the Chinese zodiac (from the ancient Greek for "cycle of animals"). As with other zodiac years, those born in a Year of the Rat are said to possess some of their animal's traits: in this case, intelligence, confidence, and a little selfishness.

Japanese Mythology

The myths told here were born on the islands of Japan, which include four major islands and more than 14,000 smaller ones. These myths are part of the Shinto religion, which had developed in Japan by 2,000 years ago or even earlier. Shinto is based on belief in immortal beings called *kami*, which can be translated as gods, goddesses, and spirits. *Kami* live in—and give life to—all things, from wind and water to mountains and rocks. Today and in the past, *kami* have been worshipped at household shrines and at public shrines, where priests lead the worship.

There are three main groups of *kami*: the heaven-living *kami*, known as Amatsukami; the earth-living *kami*, called Kunitsukami; and many more minor or local *kami*, called *ya-o-yorozu no kami* (meaning "countless *kami*"). The heavenly *kami* live in the sky, in the realm of Takamagahara. They include the sun goddess Amaterasu and the creator god Izanagi. The earthly *kami* live on or in the earth. They include Konohanasakuya-hime, the *kami* of Mount Fuji, as well as *kami* of particular places, families, ancestors, activities, or jobs.

Japanese myths explain the birth of the Japanese islands, their people, and the imperial family. The imperial family includes a long line of ruling emperors that began with Emperor Jimmu, who is said to have ruled from 660 BCE. Jimmu is believed to have been a descendant of both the sun goddess Amaterasu (opposite) and the *kami* Toyotama-hime (below). Although Jimmu cannot be proved to have existed, the events of his reign—as told in the myths—resemble real events that took place in ancient times around the great Japanese city of Nara.

For hundreds of years, Japanese myths were passed down by word of mouth, told by person to person. In the 8th century, two collections of myths were written down for the first time: in the *Kojiki* and *Nihon Shoki*. It is from these texts that we know of the *kami* Toyotama-hime, grandmother of Emperor Jimmu.

The sun goddess Amaterasu is often considered the most important *kami*. After being shamed by her brother Susanoo (see page 100), she hid in a cave. This plunged the world into terrifying darkness, until a group of *kami* persuaded Amaterasu to show herself once more.

Izanami and Izanagi

Izanami and Izanagi were sister and brother. They were the seventh generation of *kami* to come into being. When Izanami and Izanagi first opened their far-seeing eyes, there was already a cloud-crossed heaven and an ocean-covered earth. Yet no *kami* had yet created the beautiful islands of Japan.

Izanami and her brother Izanagi liked to walk on the floating bridge, named Ame-no-Ukihashi, which stretched between heaven and earth. As far as Izanami could see, there was only rippling silver sea. "Brother," said Izanami, "let us shape islands in the ocean."

"Sister," said Izanagi, waving his jewel-encrusted spear, which was named Tenkei, "let us make those islands shine like the jewels in my spear."

So Izanagi dipped his spear in the water. He stirred until the water thickened and clotted, pushing a rocky island above the waves. The sister and brother named the island Onogoroshima. Today, that island nestles between the vast islands of Honshu and Shikoku.

"Brother," said Izanami, "let us live on this island. Together, we will create children who will become the other islands of Japan."

At first, everything happened as Izanami hoped. The pair made countless children, who became the islands we know as Honshu, Shikoku, Kyushu, and many more. To give beauty to those islands, Izanami made children to live upon them, from the *kami* of mountains to the *kami* of golden, falling leaves.

Then, with an earth-shattering shriek, Izanami gave birth to the *kami* of fire, who was named Kagutsuchi. That *kami* was so fierce and flaming that his mother was killed. She descended at once to Yomi, the dark underworld of the dead.

In his furious grief, Izanagi seized his sword and beheaded Kagutsuchi. From that fiery *kami*'s body were born eight volcanoes, which spewed red-hot rock over Japan's plains. Then Izanagi rushed into Yomi, fumbling through the darkness of its winding, rocky caves. He called: "Sister! Sister, come back to me!"

"Brother," said Izanami in the blackness, "if I return to the land of the living, you must never look at me, for death has changed me."

Izanagi could not bear to never again see his sister's face, so he pulled the comb from his hair, then sparked its teeth into flame. In that glimmering light, he saw that his beautiful sister was indeed changed. Beetles crawled across her skin. Worms wriggled through her hair.

And in that same light, Izanami saw her brother's disgust. In furious shame, Izanami shouted for the darkness-dwelling demoness named Shikome. "Shikome!" cried Izanami. "Chase my brother out of Yomi!"

Izanagi ran for the light as fast as he could, but that demoness thundered close behind, her great fists yanking at his hair. Izanagi thought fast—then he hurled juicy grapes and tasty bamboo shoots over his shoulder. The distracted demoness crouched to eat.

Now Izanami called for Raijin, god of lightning, and his army of demons. "Raijin!" cried Izanami. "Teach my brother a lesson!"

Izanagi ran faster than ever, scuffing his knuckles, banging his elbows, against the rocky walls. Raijin's lightning flashed, while that army of demons bleated. Izanagi thought fast—then he hurled peaches over his shoulder. Those soft fruits had the power to protect against evil spirits. The demon army turned back.

Now Izanami gave chase to her brother. Yet, just as her fingers were grasping at his silken kimono, he scampered into the sunlight. Quick as he could, Izanagi rolled a great stone across the entrance to Yomi, shutting his sister, her demons, and all the dead, into the cave.

Behind that stone, Izanami roared with rage: "Brother, as *kami* of death, I will take one thousand souls a day to dwell with me in Yomi."

And Izanagi roared with no lesser rage: "Sister, as *kami* of life, I will give life to one thousand five hundred babies a day to dwell with me in the sunlight."

Izanami and Izanagi never met again.

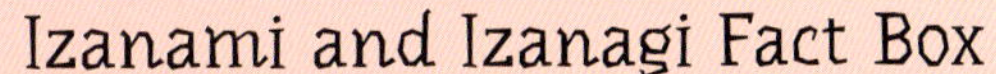

Izanami and Izanagi Fact Box

PARENTS Ame-no-Minakanushi summoned them into existence. He was one of the first *kami*, who appeared at the start of the universe.

POWERS Izanami and Izanagi have the power to create countless *kami*, lands, and living things. Through her own death, Izanami became *kami* of death, while Izanagi took the opposing role as *kami* of life.

Kami

The word *kami* is often translated into English as "spirits" or "gods." These immortal beings are part of nature and make nature. Just as nature is both beautiful and terrifying, the *kami* have both good and bad characteristics. According to tradition, there are 8 million *kami*.

FUJIN

Fierce *kami* of the wind, Fujin has a terrifying face, red hair, and green skin. He carries a bag of winds on his shoulders. He is often seen with his brother Raijin, god of storms, thunder, and lightning.

AME-NO-UZUME

Ame-no-Uzume is *kami* of dawn, laughter, dancers, and other performers. She is famed for using her comical dancing to entice the sun *kami* Amaterasu (see page 97) out of her cave. Ame-no-Uzume's husband is Sarutahiko Okami, leader of the earthly *kami*.

SUSANOO

A *kami* who can be both good and bad, heroic and violent, Susanoo is god of the sea. His quick-tempered nature makes him stormy and unpredictable. His children include the *kami* of harvest, named Toshigami, and the *kami* of rice, named Ukanomitama.

KONOHANASAKUYA-HIME

This *kami* is goddess of volcanoes, including Mount Fuji, the active volcano close to today's Japanese capital, Tokyo. It is believed that Konohanasakuya prevents Fuji from erupting. She is also *kami* of blossoms, including cherry blossom, Japan's national flower.

TOYOTAMA-HIME

Toyotama was the daughter of a dragon water *kami* named Watatsumi. She married the human prince Hoori, but after giving birth to a son, she turned into a crocodile-like dragon and disappeared. Her son's son, known as Jimmu, became Japan's legendary first emperor.

TSUKUYOMI

Tsukuyomi is *kami* of the moon. Locked in an unhappy marriage with the sun goddess Amaterasu (see page 97), he spends his time following her across the sky.

Tsukuyomi Fact Box

MOTHER Izanami, *kami* of creation and death

FATHER Izanagi, *kami* of creation and life. Tsukuyomi was born when Izanagi washed his right eye, Amaterasu from Izanagi's left eye, and their brother Susanoo from Izanagi's nose.

POWERS A lover of order and ritual, Tsukuyomi killed the *kami* of food because of her table manners. This led to a bitter argument with Amaterasu, who refused to be in the same part of the sky with him, creating the separation of day and night.

Hindu Mythology

Hindu mythology is a vast collection of stories about the loves and battles, creations and adventures, of the gods and goddesses of the Hindu religion. These stories have been passed down to us in ancient texts such as the Vedas, which were first written down by around 500 BCE but were passed on orally—by memory, from person to person—for at least a thousand years before. Hinduism developed in India from earlier South Asian religious beliefs. By around 500 BCE, Hinduism had started to take the form we recognize. Today, Hinduism has around 1.2 billion believers, the majority in India but many living all across the world.

Hindu gods and goddesses can be worshipped at public temples, where people pray and take part in rituals, as well as at household shrines. While there are hundreds of Hindu gods and goddesses, believers may worship only one deity or a small group of deities that are important to them. Some Hindus worship the gods Vishnu or Shiva as the supreme god, creator of all. Others believe that the supreme creator was a mother goddess named Shakti, who takes the form of female goddesses including Parvati, Lakshmi, and Durga. Many Hindus consider all gods and goddesses to be aspects of one creative force, called the Brahman.

In Hindu belief, each person has four goals in life: *dharma* (leading a good life), *kama* (finding love and enjoyment), *artha* (finding purpose through work), and *moksha* (finding freedom through spiritual knowledge). *Moksha* is freedom from *samsara*, which is the cycle of life, death, and rebirth, in which each soul is reborn in a new body after death. Through meeting these four goals, a soul will not be reborn once more, but will become one with the supreme god or Brahman.

Ganesha is the god of new beginnings, good luck, and intelligence. His elephant's head symbolizes his wisdom, since elephants are believed to be intelligent animals. However, the god was born with a human head, which was removed by an angry Shiva then replaced with the first head that Shiva found.

One of the most widely worshipped Hindu goddesses, Parvati is goddess of motherhood, energy, and creativity. She is the wife of Shiva and mother of Ganesha and Kartikeya, god of war (shown here). She is often depicted riding a lion, which symbolizes her fierce willingness to fight for justice.

Rama's Rescue

Rama was prince of Ayodhya in northern India. The prince was as human as you or I, his brown skin as soft, his life as fragile as ours. Yet Rama was extraordinary, for he loved his wife Sita more than life itself. For her part, Sita was devoted to Rama. The pair's heavenly love should have been a blessing for all hearts. Yet the heart of the ten-headed demon king Ravana was cruel. He determined to destroy the love of Rama and Sita.

Using all of his ten heads, Ravana thought up an evil plan. Then he leaped into his chariot, grasping the reins with his twenty arms, and flew to the home of his uncle Maricha. This uncle was a dark-hearted, flesh-eating, blood-drinking demon. At Ravana's request, Maricha disguised himself as a golden deer with dappled spots of silver, moonstone, amethyst, and sapphire.

As swiftly as only evil can travel, that beautiful deer was soon trotting past Sita. The lovely princess was walking in the Dandaka Forest with her husband and her husband's loyal brother, who was named Lakshmana.

"Oh, see that pretty deer, Rama!" cried Sita as the deer darted into the darkness beneath the twisting branches. She plucked a fruit from a jujube tree. "Will you offer this jujube so the deer will play with us?"

"I will, my love," cried Rama as he ran in pursuit of the quick-hoofed deer.

Yet Maricha the deer sped on, faster and faster, with Rama at his heels, farther and farther from Sita and Lakshmana. And as Maricha bounded between the black trunks, he shouted in a voice that sounded like Rama's: "Lakshmana, help me! Help!"

At once, Lakshmana ran in his brother's footsteps, leaving Sita alone in the forest. As she looked nervously around her, a wandering holy man appeared among the trees. "Can you spare me a little food and water, princess?" asked the holy man, as he shuffled close to Sita.

Sita's kind heart was shaping her lips to answer, when the holy man took his true form: the demon Ravana. Fast as a falcon, Ravana snatched Sita away to his kingdom of Lanka, which lay on an island across the sea.

Rama Fact Box

MOTHER	Queen Kausalya of Ayodhya
FATHER	King Dasharatha of Ayodhya
POWERS	Rama's loving and virtuous human life sets an example for believers to follow. He represents the goal of *dharma* (leading a good life). He is also an avatar (the physical form, made flesh and blood on earth) of the great god Vishnu.

Ravana imprisoned Sita in a grove of red-flowered ashoka trees. Day and night, Sita was surrounded by demon warriors with sharp fangs and sharper swords. Night and day, Ravana tried to persuade Sita to marry him, using words of sickly sweetness and gifts of glittering gold. Yet Sita's heart stayed true to Rama.

Rama and Lakshmana soon realized they had been tricked by that demon deer. Rama shot an arrow from his bow, killing Maricha stone dead. Then the brothers went in search of the monkey-faced god Hanuman, who led a fierce army of monkeys. With Hanuman's help, the brothers hoped they could defeat Ravana and rescue Sita.

Kind-hearted Hanuman was soon persuaded to help the brothers, so soon that—before the sun had set—Rama, Lakshmana, and Hanuman were leading an army of monkeys to the coast. There they gazed across the blue sea to the island of Lanka. But before Rama could wonder how to cross those waves, the monkeys Nala and Nila set to work with hoots and leaps. They threw rocks into the water, making a bridge.

So, on Lanka's shore, Rama's monkey army met Ravana's demon army. The two forces battled for day after day, with monkeys pulling demons' hair and demons pulling monkeys' tails. Those two armies would still be battling today, but the god Vishnu looked down upon Rama, seeing into his heart to the selfless love that bloomed like a lotus. Vishnu filled Rama with his power, making him a god.

Now Rama's skin shone as blue as the sea and sky. His arms strong as the mountains, his eyes far-seeing, Rama climbed onto Hanuman's shoulders. He loosed an arrow that pierced Ravana's bitter heart.

As the demon warriors scuttled away, Sita ran to Rama, scattering scarlet ashoka petals behind her. At the moment that Sita hugged her husband to her heart, she became the goddess of devotion. And from that day forward, the loving pair were never parted again.

Gods and Goddesses

In temples and shrines, Hindu gods and goddesses are often depicted with several arms as a symbol of their great power and multiple abilities. Some deities are depicted with blue skin, which represents their link with the vastness of the universe, visible to human eyes as blue sky and sea.

SARASWATI

Saraswati is goddess of knowledge, language, poetry, and music. In her four arms she holds a book (representing learning), prayer beads (representing spirituality), a water pot (representing purity), and a musical instrument called a *veena* (representing creativity). She rides a white swan and dresses in white, a shade linked with purity and truth.

LAKSHMI

Goddess of beauty, power, and wealth, Lakshmi is usually shown with lotus flowers, which represent enlightenment—the highest spiritual state, of total understanding. Lakshmi's four arms represent a Hindu's four goals: *dharma*, *kama*, *artha*, and *moksha* (see page 102).

VISHNU

Vishnu is protector of goodness and defender of the universe. He holds a conch shell (symbolizing the spiraling cycle of life and death), war discus (symbolizing that he will use force to defeat evil), club (symbolizing his authority), and lotus flower. Vishnu's wife is the goddess Lakshmi.

SHIVA

In his gentler form, Shiva is god of meditation and yoga, which is a system of physical and mental exercises aimed at controlling the body, mind, and spirit. In Shiva's fiercer aspect, he is a killer of demons. On his forehead is a third eye, which sees all evil, turning it to dust.

KRISHNA

One of the most widely worshipped Hindu deities, Krishna is god of kindness, gentleness, and love. He is often depicted with the Indian flute called a *bansuri*, which he played for his love, the goddess Radha.

KALI

Goddess of time, death, and destruction, Kali often holds a *khadga* (curving sword), severed head, and a bowl to catch the head's dripping blood. The sword represents spiritual knowledge, while the head represents ignorance, which must be destroyed by knowledge to gain release from the cycle of death and rebirth.

Kali Fact Box

PARENTS Kali was born when Parvati (goddess of motherhood) shed her dark skin. Kali (which means "the dark one") became the creative goddess's fiercer self.

POWERS Although Kali is a terrifying destroyer of evil, she is also a defender of innocence. She is able to create by destroying the evil and decay that plague the world. She gives *moksha* (freedom from the cycle of rebirth) to those who achieve true knowledge.

Mount Meru

In Hinduism, a holy mountain named Meru lies at the middle of the universe. Mount Meru is a link between earth and heaven. Gods and goddesses are often found on the mountain's slopes, with their palaces on its summit.

Mount Meru is not usually believed to be a "real" geographical place, but it has great emotional importance to Hindus: Its peak symbolizes a believer's journey to a higher spiritual state. Many Hindu temples are designed to remind worshippers of Mount Meru by having a mountain-shaped tower called a *shikhara*. Mount Meru is also central to the universes of the Buddhist and Jain religions, which were born in ancient India.

Meru means "high" in the ancient South Asian language called Sanskrit. It is believed to be not only the tallest mountain on earth, but to dwarf all other possible mountains. Around Mount Meru's base is the earth inhabited by humans, which lies within seven encircling seas. The holy River Ganges flows from Mount Meru, becoming four rivers that give life—both physical and spiritual—to the land.

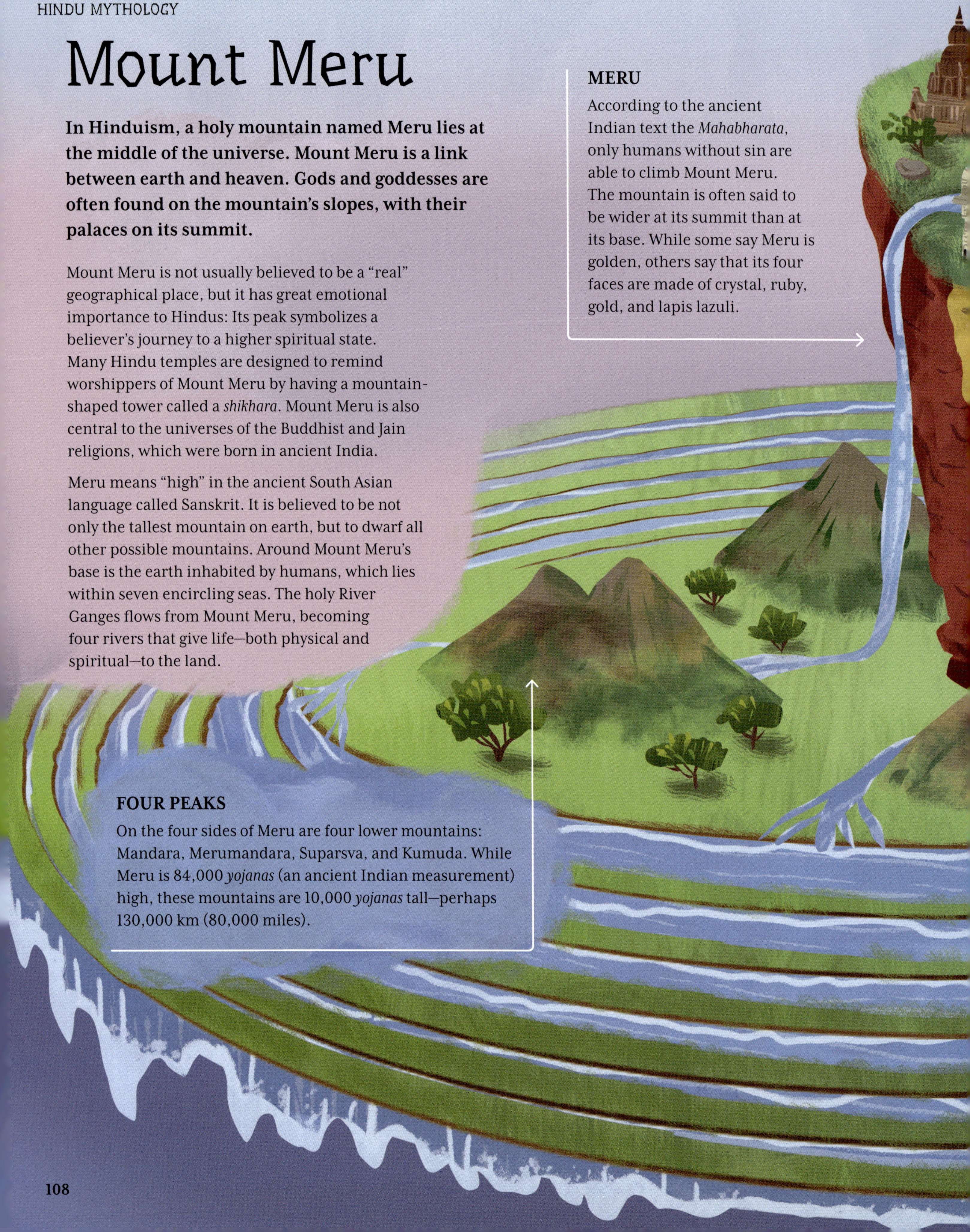

MERU

According to the ancient Indian text the *Mahabharata*, only humans without sin are able to climb Mount Meru. The mountain is often said to be wider at its summit than at its base. While some say Meru is golden, others say that its four faces are made of crystal, ruby, gold, and lapis lazuli.

FOUR PEAKS

On the four sides of Meru are four lower mountains: Mandara, Merumandara, Suparsva, and Kumuda. While Meru is 84,000 *yojanas* (an ancient Indian measurement) high, these mountains are 10,000 *yojanas* tall—perhaps 130,000 km (80,000 miles).

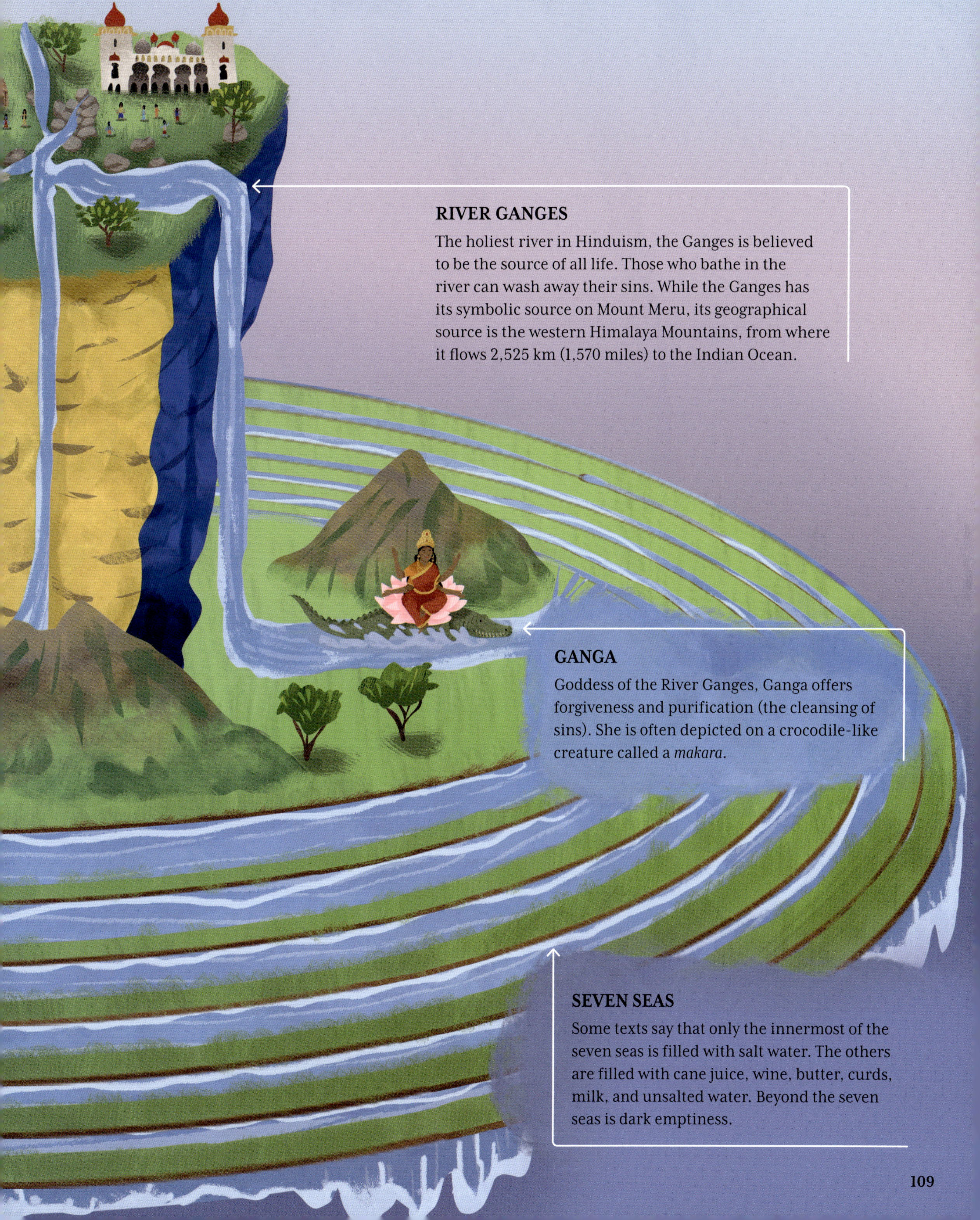

RIVER GANGES

The holiest river in Hinduism, the Ganges is believed to be the source of all life. Those who bathe in the river can wash away their sins. While the Ganges has its symbolic source on Mount Meru, its geographical source is the western Himalaya Mountains, from where it flows 2,525 km (1,570 miles) to the Indian Ocean.

GANGA

Goddess of the River Ganges, Ganga offers forgiveness and purification (the cleansing of sins). She is often depicted on a crocodile-like creature called a *makara*.

SEVEN SEAS

Some texts say that only the innermost of the seven seas is filled with salt water. The others are filled with cane juice, wine, butter, curds, milk, and unsalted water. Beyond the seven seas is dark emptiness.

Durga's Battle

There was once a demon named Mahishasura. This demon was the child of demons, his father a demon with a human shape and his mother with buffalo shape. This meant Mahishasura was half-buffalo, with a human head but shining hooves. Yet that destructive demon could take the shape of any animal to cause chaos with scratching claws or flapping wings. And Mahishasura had a plan to destroy all that was good.

The first part of Mahishasura's plan was this: For three years, he sat under a tree and prayed to Brahma, one of the great gods who created the universe. At last, just when Mahishasura was losing patience, Brahma called: "Mahishasura, I will reward you for your devotion. Ask me for anything you want!"

"I ask only that no god or man will ever kill me," said Mahishasura with a sly kick of his hooves.

"Your wish is granted," said Brahma, the all-knowing.

Now that Mahishasura believed he was immortal, he wasted no time in wreaking havoc. In buffalo form, he trampled farms, churned rivers into floods, and leaped across the heavens, smashing the palaces on Mount Meru.

Brahma called ten of the gods to him, among the snow-capped peaks of the Himalayas: Shiva, Vishnu, Yama, Vayu, Surya, Tvashta, Ganesha, Indra, Varuna, and Himavan. "Mahishasura thinks he is invincible," said Brahma, "but in his arrogance he forgets that not only gods and men can wield weapons. We will make a powerful goddess to defeat him."

So the gods willed a goddess into existence. That tall goddess was fierce eyed and ten armed. She spoke at once, with a voice that shook the snow from the mountains: "My name is Durga, which means undefeatable."

Then the gods gave Durga one weapon for each of her ten hands. Shiva gave a three-pronged trident, Vishnu gave a sharp-edged discus, Yama gave a sword, Vayu gave a bow, and Surya gave an arrow. Tvashta gave a heavy mace, while Ganesha gave a rope looped into a noose. Indra gave a *vajra*, which could send thunderbolts flying. Varuna gave a conch shell, which—when blown into—made a deafening, flattening, shattering sound. Finally, Brahma gave a lotus flower, which offered the greatest weapon of all: wisdom.

Now Durga had no free hand to take a weapon from Himavan, who was god of the Himalayas. Yet Himavan had a better idea: He summoned a lion, which crouched at Durga's feet so she could climb onto his furry back.

"I will defeat that dreadful demon," called Durga as she galloped to the valley where Mahishasura, in his buffalo form, was grazing on the lentil crop.

When Mahishasura saw Durga, he took his almost-human form, his moustache and hooves shining. "Beautiful goddess," he said slyly, "I am quivering with astonishment at your loveliness. Will you marry me?"

For answer, Durga blew into her conch shell. Shaking almost to breaking, Mahishasura managed to transform into buffalo form. He charged at Durga, but her lion leaped aside. Now Mahishasura transformed into a tiger that sprang and bit. Durga unleashed thunderbolts from her *vajra*, hurling the demon backward. But he became a hefty elephant. Durga looped her rope around his trunk, yet Mahishasura became a snake to slither out of the wide noose.

Durga fired an arrow at wriggling Mahishasura, but he only became a falcon to flap away. Now Durga hurled her discus into the air, shaving the demon's feathers, yet he landed among the neem trees and became a bear. Galloping on her tireless lion, Durga raced for that heavy beast. Just as Durga was about to swipe Mahishasura's massive head with her mace, he shrank into a tiny scorpion. Durga drew her sword at once, but the scorpion scuttled into the grass.

Durga leaped off her lion, then stamped and stomped, hoping to squash the eight-legged demon. Quick-thinking Mahishasura took his human form once more. Standing almost within Durga's reach, he twirled his moustache.

Durga Fact Box

PARENTS	Brahma and other male gods
POWERS	Perhaps the most powerful goddess of all, Durga is goddess of strength and protection. She unleashes her fierce energy to destroy evil and free the innocent.

The goddess had only two weapons left: her trident and, of course, her wisdom. She thought hard. And then, just as Mahishasura was changing back into buffalo form, she saw her chance. While the demon's head was still human, but his tail twitched and his legs bristled, all his energy was engaged in his transformation. He was at his weakest.

Durga jabbed with her trident. She pierced the demon's hairy flesh.

Mahishasura gave a shriek of anger that shook Mount Meru itself. Then the demon was dead.

Durga's battle was won.

Aboriginal Australian Mythology

Aboriginal Australians have lived on the vast continent of Australia for at least 50,000 years. The term Aboriginal comes from the Latin words for "from the beginning." The term includes many different Aboriginal Australian peoples, from the Tiwi of northern Australia to the Kulin of the south. Over thousands of years, these peoples developed complex cultures and religious beliefs, as well as more than 300 languages. The arrival of Europeans on the continent, from 1606, brought disaster to Aboriginal lives and traditions.

Today, many Aboriginal Australians strive to preserve and protect traditions such as their mythology. The myths told and represented here belong to the Aboriginal Australian peoples who passed them down, from person to person, over thousands of years, and will continue to pass them to future generations. The myths are described and depicted here with gratitude.

Each Aboriginal Australian people has its own mythology about different spirits, who are often called ancestral beings. Yet key religious and spiritual beliefs are shared by most peoples. At the heart of these beliefs is the Dreamtime, the long-ago period when ancestral beings shaped the landscape. Yet the Dreamtime is also the present and future, because it shows us how to live today and how to protect nature for tomorrow. Ancestral beings are not worshipped in temples, but some places—including waterholes, mountains, and rocks—are sacred because of their link with the spirits. The telling of myths about the Dreamtime—often at gatherings called corroborees—is an essential way to connect with ancestral beings and with nature.

A yawkyawk is a female ancestral being that protects the pools and streams of the Kuninjku people of northern Australia. In addition to its fish-woman form, a yawkyawk can transform into a dragonfly, freshwater turtle, or crocodile.

The Anindilyakwa people of northeastern Australia tell of an ancestral being named Ipilja-ipilja. A huge and hairy gecko, Ipilja-ipilja creates rain by sucking water from the swamp where he lives, then spitting it into the sky. When he is pleased, he roars to make thunder.

The Rainbow Serpent

Many Aboriginal Australian peoples tell of a creator spirit known in English as the Rainbow Serpent or Rainbow Snake. This ancestral being shaped the land and created plants and animals. For many peoples, the Rainbow Serpent has power over rain and waterholes. Particularly in Australia's dry, desert interior, water is the most precious resource of all.

The Rainbow Serpent is called by different names by different peoples. The Warramunga people of northern Australia call the spirit Wollunqua, yet try not to say the name out loud due to the ancestral being's great power. For the Warramunga, the serpent emerged from the ground at the waterhole called Kadjinara in the Murchison Range, then wriggled far to the west. The spirit is so long that his tail never left Kadjinara.

The Noongar, whose lands are on the southwestern coast of Australia, call the Rainbow Serpent: Wagyl. Wagyl created rivers and landforms throughout Noongar lands. His wrigglings created the Swan and Canning Rivers, with his swift turns shaping sharp bends. On the coast near today's Fremantle, Wagyl's battle with a crocodile separated the rivers' fresh water from sea water. Then Wagyl rested at the base of Mount Eliza, in today's Perth, making this a sacred site, known as Gooninup, for the Noongar peoples.

As Wagyl continued to slither over the land, he formed the great rocks, ridges, and valleys of the Porongurup and Darling Ranges. Wagyl's droppings made piles of pebbles. Where Wagyl writhed across gravelly ground, he scraped off his scales, which grew and bloomed into woods and forests. At last, Wagyl named the Noongar people as guardians of this land.

For the Lardil people of Mornington Island in northern Australia, the Rainbow Serpent is called Goorialla. The Lardil artist and storyteller Dick Roughsey described how, after shaping the landscape, Goorialla made a great flood. Two brothers asked Goorialla for shelter, so he swallowed them. The brothers escaped from Goorialla's stomach as rainbow lorikeets, which have feathers of green, blue, red, and yellow.

The Kuninjku people of northern Australia tell similar stories of swallowing and rebirth. For them, the Rainbow Serpent is named Ngalyod. When traditional laws are broken, Ngalyod swallows people with floods that he created, then spits them out as new beings. At these times, the spirit's fury makes the startling flash of lightning and the deep rumble of thunder.

For some Aboriginal Australian peoples, the Rainbow Serpent is male, while for others this ancestral being is female, the great mother of all. For the Murinbata of northern Australia, the Rainbow Serpent, called Kunmanggur, is both male and female.

Many peoples describe the Rainbow Serpent as having scales of glittering brightness and every shade of the rainbow. The ancestral being is associated with the sparkling rainbows that can be seen in waterfalls or as sunlight falls on water. For Aboriginal peoples across Australia, when a bright rainbow is seen arching across the sky, it is said to be the Rainbow Serpent making its way from waterhole to waterhole. The spirit feeds these sacred waterholes so that they never dry up, not even in the longest and thirstiest drought. For those who know the land well enough to find these waterholes, the Rainbow Serpent offers both water and life.

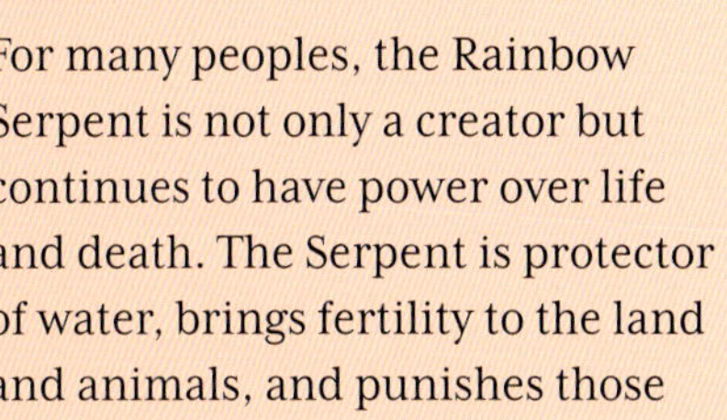

Rainbow Serpent Fact Box

PARENTS None

POWERS For many peoples, the Rainbow Serpent is not only a creator but continues to have power over life and death. The Serpent is protector of water, brings fertility to the land and animals, and punishes those who break traditional laws.

Astronomy

For thousands of years, Aboriginal Australians have used the position and movement of the sun, moon, planets, and stars to keep calendars and to navigate across their continent. Just as Western astronomy has named star patterns—called constellations—in the night sky, Aboriginal Australians have named the animals and objects they saw in the southern sky.

EMU

The shape of Emu is made not by stars but by dark nebulae (clouds of dust and gas) that block our view of the bright stripe of stars called the Milky Way. Emu's head is the Coalsack Nebula, while its body and legs are the dark band of cloud called the Great Rift.

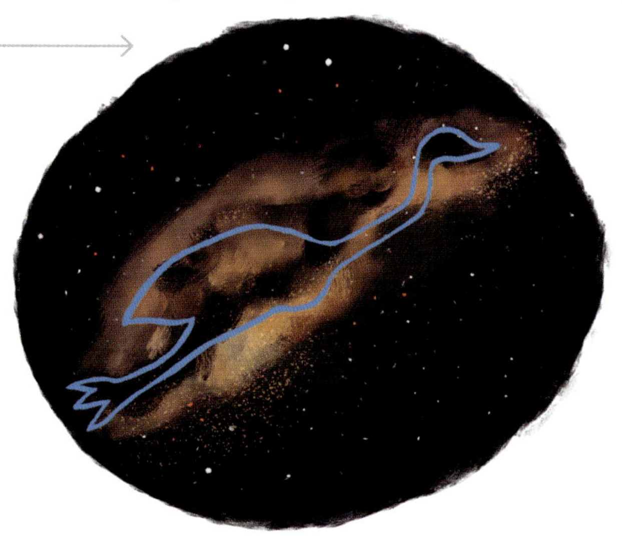

BAHLOO

Among most Aboriginal Australian peoples, the moon is a male spirit. The Gamilaraay people of eastern Australia call this spirit Bahloo. The female sun spirit, Yhi, asked to be Bahloo's companion, but he refused her. Ever since, the sun has chased the moon across the sky. When she catches him, we see an eclipse, which—in scientific terms—is when the moon passes in front of the sun, or the earth's shadow falls on the full moon.

CANOE

While ancient Greek astronomers saw the Orion constellation as a hunter with three stars in his belt, the Yolngu people of northern Australia see it as a canoe carrying three brothers. The brothers were turned into stars by the sun-woman as punishment for eating a forbidden sawfish, which—at the end of a bright fishing line—became the Orion Nebula.

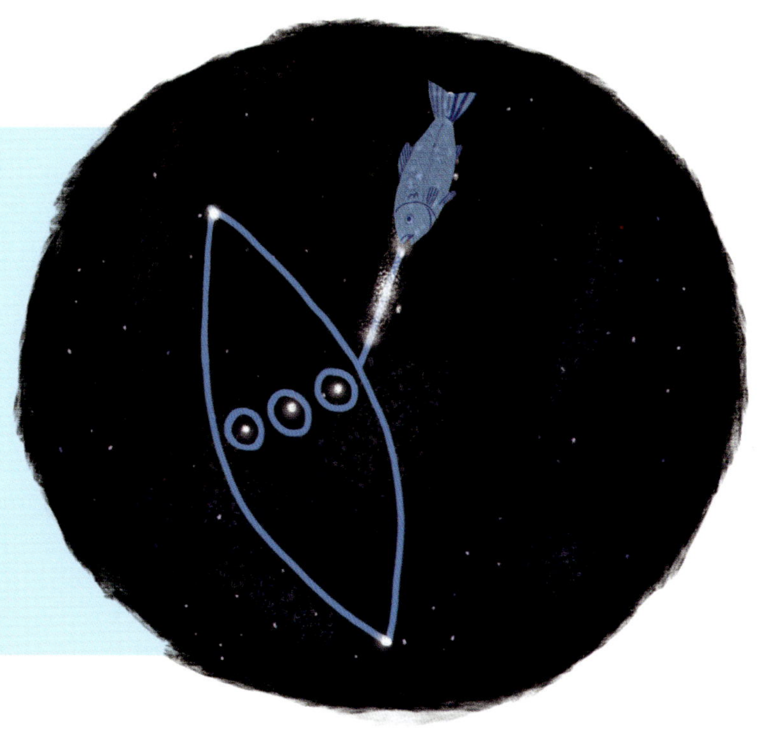

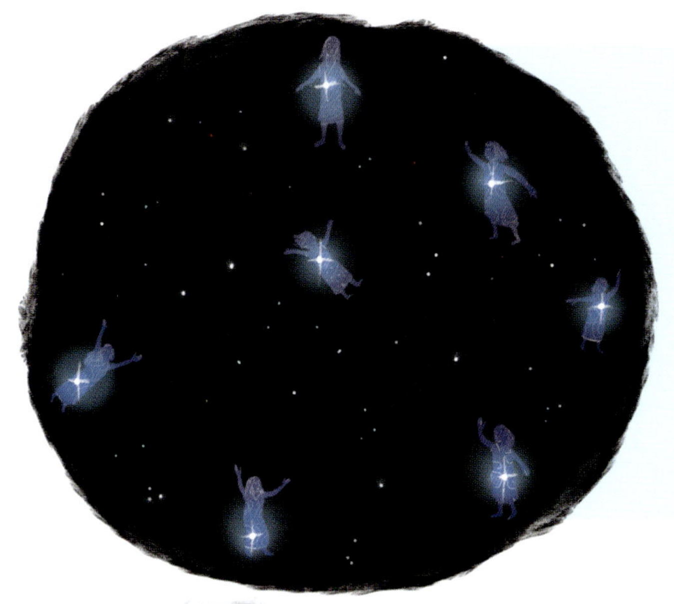

SEVEN SISTERS

Just as ancient Greeks saw the star cluster M45 as seven sisters called the Pleiades, many Aboriginal Australian peoples also see seven sisters. In the Kimberley area of northwestern Australia, people say the sisters were chased into the sky by an eagle-hawk.

BUNJIL

Among the Kulin people of southern Australia, the creator spirit Bunjil was a wedge-tailed eagle. After creating the land and rivers, he called for winds. Yet the winds were so strong that Bunjil was blown into the sky, becoming the bright star known to Western astronomers as Altair, in the constellation of Aquila (Latin for "eagle").

WURIUPRANILI

Most Aboriginal Australian peoples see the sun as a female spirit. The Tiwi people of northern Australia call the sun-woman Wuriupranili. Each day, she carries a flaming branch of stringybark tree across the sky, from east to west.

Wuriupranili Fact Box

PARENTS None

POWERS Each morning, after Wuriupranili lights her torch, she paints her skin with red pigment. When the pigment rubs off on the clouds, she creates a beautiful sunrise. At nightfall, she puts out her torch and reapplies her pigment, creating sunset. During the night, she makes her dangerous way through underground tunnels to her eastern camp.

Māori Mythology

Māori mythology tells of the creation of the universe by gods, goddesses, and spirits known as *atuas*. It explains how nature took the form we know, from why the moon appears to change shape to why there are fish in the sea. It also explains the rules and activities of human society, from how humans gained the skill of fire-making to the rituals around canoe-carving. Many exciting myths are about the adventures of demi-gods: heroes who are born human but have supernatural powers. Among the most famed of these heroes are Rātā (opposite) and Māui (see page 124). These heroes are a bridge between the world of humans and the world of *atuas*. With their flaws and mistakes, the demi-gods offer us valuable lessons.

Between around 1300 and 1350, Māori arrived in New Zealand by canoe from Polynesian islands around 3,000 km (1,900 miles) to the northeast. The voyagers brought the beliefs and mythology of their Polynesian homeland. In the new setting, the settlers' mythology adapted and developed. Yet it continued to share gods, ideas, and stories with the mythology of Polynesia. Other traditions brought from Polynesia but given new life in New Zealand included styles of music, dance, poetry, art, and skin tattooing, known in the Māori language as *ta moko*.

From the beginning, Māori myths were passed down orally. They were told as stories, which were performed on dark nights for entertainment, teaching, and spiritual wellbeing. The myths were also told as poetry, which was sung or chanted. Over time, different *iwi* (tribes) developed different versions of each myth. Although the myths were first written down in the 19th century, they continued to be performed. Today, many Māori follow another religion, such as Christianity, or no religion. However, the traditional Māori religion still forms part of many people's beliefs. Many other people treasure Māori mythology as a rich part of their culture.

Tangaroa is *atua* of the sea, rivers, and lakes. His son Punga is the ancestor of sharks and their relatives the rays. His grandson Ikatere is the ancestor of all other fish.

The hero Rātā set out to carve a canoe. He cut down a forest tree, then went home for the night. In the morning, he found the tree standing upright once more. This happened again and again, until the bird-like *hākuturi*, guardians of the forest, explained to Rātā that he had failed to perform the proper rituals before felling the tree.

Rangi and Papa

The first *atuas* were Rangi and Papa. Rangi was *atua* of the sky, while Papa was *atua* of the earth. The loving pair were husband and wife. They clung together, locked constantly in a tight cuddle, until their sons decided to take action.

Rangi and Papa had many sons, including Tāne, Tawhirimatea, Tumatauenga, Haumia, Tangaroa (see page 118), and Rongo (see page 122). Since Rangi and Papa pressed together so tightly, the boys could live only in the dark crevices between their parents. All of the universe was in darkness, with no room for creation. The brothers could not take their places as *atuas* of the natural world.

The fiercest son, Tumatauenga, suggested killing their parents so the brothers could live in the light. Tāne disagreed. He suggested a gentler path to freedom: that they push their parents apart, pressing Rangi high and Papa far below. So the brothers strained with their strong arms to push their parents apart. At last, Tāne was successful when he tried a different method: He lay on his back and pushed with his legs instead.

TUMATAUENGA

The fierce *atua* of war and hunting, Tumatauenga felt no guilt for suggesting the murder of his parents. In fact, he was so angry at his gentler brothers, the *atuas* of nature, that he went to war with them. His attitude continues to influence human actions: He is the reason why humans sometimes treat the sea and land with disrespect.

RANGI

Wailing with sorrow, Rangi was pushed away from his beloved wife. To this day, Rangi and Papa continue to long for each other. Rangi's tears fall to earth as rain. Papa's sighs of grief rise from the earth as mist.

TAWHIRIMATEA

This *atua* was the only son of Rangi and Papa who did not want to tear them apart. *Atua* of weather, he joined his father in the sky. Then he showed his anger at his brothers by churning Tangaroa's sea with storms and by blowing down the trees of Tāne's forests.

TĀNE

Tāne is *atua* of forests and birds. After separating his parents, he threw the moon, sun, and stars into the sky so his father would be appropriately dressed. Some myths tell us that Tāne went on to make the first human man and woman.

PAPA

Papa's youngest son was still in her belly when she was pushed away from Rangi. She keeps that son, called Ruaumoko, inside her today, so she is not alone. When Ruaumoko kicks, the earth shakes, since he is *atua* of earthquakes.

HAUMIA

While Haumia's brother Rongo became *atua* of the plants grown by farmers, Haumia became *atua* of wild plants that can be eaten. Among these was the bracken fern, which has edible rootstalks. Papa hid Haumia and Rongo in the ground to protect them from Tawhirimatea's storms.

Atuas

The Māori word for gods, goddesses, and spirits is *atuas*. The word means "power." *Atuas* are present in all things, from rainbows to the plants grown by farmers. Just as there are troubles in human life, from storms to illness, the *atuas* are capable of cruelty as well as kindness.

RONGO

God of farming, Rongo takes care of crops. In the days before Europeans reached New Zealand, key crops included *kumara* (sweet potato), *uwhi* (yam), *ti* (cordyline), and *hue* (calabash gourds), most of them brought to the islands by Māori.

WHAITIRI

This fearsome *atua* is goddess of thunder. She descended from the sky to marry a mortal man named Kaitangata, who complained that her skin was like the wind and her heart was cold as ice. The furious *atua* returned to the sky in a dark cloud.

UENUKU

This *atua* of rainbows was also associated with war. It was said that, if a war party was first seen under the arch of a rainbow, they would be defeated. Yet if they appeared to left or right of a rainbow, they would be victorious.

HINA

Atua of the moon, Hina is usually described as the older sister of Māui (see page 124). As Hinatea ("Fair Hina"), she is *atua* of the full moon, while as Hinauri ("Dark Hina"), she is *atua* of the new moon. Initially, she was only Hinatea, but after Māui turned her husband into a dog, she showed herself as Hinauri.

TAMANUITERA

Tamanuitera is *atua* of the sun. He has two wives: Hineraumati, *atua* of summer; and Hinetakurua, *atua* of winter. In the beginning, Tamanuitera journeyed too quickly across the sky, so Māui tied ropes to him to hold him back. These ropes can be seen as the sun's rays.

WHIRO

Whiro is *atua* of darkness, sickness, death, and evil. He lives in the underworld, where he devours the bodies of the dead. He can take the form of a lizard, which led to people avoiding lizards.

Whiro Fact Box

MOTHER	Papa
FATHER	Rangi
POWERS	Whiro is responsible for every disease and illness that troubles humans. He is also responsible for all the evil that humans think and do. In addition, he commands biting insects, reptiles, bats, and birds that eat carrion (dead animals), including the kahu and kea.

Māui Brings Fire

Long ago, humans did not know how to make fire. The *atuas* were generous, so they gave every home a fire for cooking *kumara* and warming toes. As long as Māori did not let their fires go out, they would always have food and warmth. Yet that trickster Māui wanted more for himself and for all humans. He wanted to know how fire was made.

One moonless night, as everyone slept beneath their blankets, Māui crept through every village, every home. In his hands, he held a gourd of water. And he poured that water onto every fire, until each blaze was only blackened, steaming sticks.

When the people woke, they were frightened and cold. Māui's mother Taranga gathered the shivering Māori around her. She was their chief, their *rangatira*. Taranga had a strong suspicion that her smirking son had something to do with this disaster.

"Māui," ordered Taranga, "go straight to the *atua* Mahuika. She is guardian of fire. Beg her for one of her flaming fingernails so we can relight our fires."

This had been Māui's plan all along. Yet he respectfully performed a *hongi*, pressing his nose to his mother's to exchange the breath of life, then he set off for the home of Mahuika.

Māui strode through the forest, where his only company was the fluttering wings of *piwakawakas*. He trudged beside rivers, where scaly *kokopu* splashed from the clear water. At last, Māui came to a mountain that belched steam and sparks into the sky. He knew that Mahuika lived in the pit of this volcano.

Up, up, up climbed Māui, past spewed lava that glowed with Mahuika's furious heat. Then—when he reached the volcano's rim and could stare into the stinking, steaming pit—he picked his way down, down, down.

"What do you want, Māui?" came a crackling voice.

He turned to face Mahuika. He pressed a hand to his startled eyes! For that *atua* blazed and flamed.

Yet Māui dared to speak to the scorching *atua*. "My people's fires have gone out. I want to know the secret of making fire," he said bravely.

"That secret belongs to the *atuas*, not to humans," sizzled Mahuika. "But I can give one of my fingernails to relight your fires." With that, she flicked a flaming fingernail at Māui.

Māui let the fingernail fall at his feet. Then, using nothing but his bare, soft toes, he stamped on it until the flame was extinguished.

"What are you doing?" snapped Mahuika. "I'll give you one more chance." She tossed him another fiery fingernail.

Again, Māui stamped on the flame. This was too much for Mahuika, who let out a scream and a shimmer of sparks. At once, Māui turned himself into a *kāhu* bird and flapped fast. He flew into the sky not a moment too soon, as red-hot rock, boiling and bubbling, surged up the throat of the volcano. And the volcano spat that lava far and wide. It surged down the slopes, setting light to grass and trees, nests and burrows.

Now Māui prayed to Tawhirimatea, *atua* of weather, and Whaitiri, *atua* of thunder. Hearing his pleas, those *atuas* sent a storm of rain to quench Mahuika's wildfire.

Māui, still winged and beaked, landed on the branch of a *mahoe* tree. But now flaming Mahuika appeared on the rim of the volcano. With a snap and a whistle, she hurled a fingernail at Māui's feathers. He flapped into the air as that bright fingernail fell into the *mahoe* tree.

Now a strange thing happened. The tree swallowed the flame, like a kiwi bird swallows a seed. Now the *mahoe* held the secret of fire.

Taking his human form once more, Māui snapped dry branches from the *mahoe* and carried them home. There he showed his people how to rub the sticks together until they showered sparks onto dry moss. When the moss was burning well, he added sticks from *totara* and *patete* trees until the fire was blazing.

Now humans knew the secret of fire.

Māui Fact Box

MOTHER	Taranga, a human woman
FATHER	Makeatutara, a guardian of the underworld
POWERS	Although he is the son of a human woman, Māui possesses supernatural powers. He can take the form of birds such as the *kāhu* (swamp harrier) and *kereru* (New Zealand pigeon). He also has exceptional cleverness, strength, and bravery.

Glossary

Aesir
A clan of Norse gods and goddesses.

ajogun
In Yoruba belief, a spirit that holds a destructive force of nature.

amulet
An ornament that is believed to give protection against misfortune.

ancestor
A person, such as a great-great-grandparent, from whom one is descended.

ancestral being
A god, goddess, or spirit who is an ancestor of people living today.

Arctic
The region around the North Pole where the sea and land are covered by ice for part or all of the year.

astronomy
The study of space, planets, moons, and stars.

atua
A god, goddess, or spirit of Māori and other Polynesian peoples.

Buddhism
A religion and philosophy based on the teachings of Siddhartha Gautama, also called the Buddha ("awakened one"), who lived in South Asia in the 6th or 5th century BCE.

Celt
A member of a group of peoples who spoke Celtic languages and, by 275 BCE, were living across a region from modern-day Ireland in the west to modern-day Turkey in the east.

civilization
A complex society, usually with cities, laws, and arts.

Confucianism
A set of ideas for leading a good life, based on the teachings of the Chinese thinker Confucius (c. 551–479 BCE).

convert
To change one's religious beliefs.

custom
A traditional way of doing something.

Daoism
A philosophy and religion that took shape in China between 450 and 300 BCE, based on the idea of living in harmony with nature and each other.

deify
To start to worship a human as a god or goddess.

deity
A god, goddess, or other immortal being that is worshipped.

demi-god
A being, often the child of a god and a human, that has more power than a human but less than a god.

demon
An evil spirit.

dragon
A mythical creature with scales and sometimes wings. In European mythology, dragons bring chaos, but in East Asia, dragons usually bring good luck.

Dreamtime
In Aboriginal Australian belief, a time in the past when spirits shaped the landscape. The Dreamtime is also the present and future, as it shows us how to live today and tomorrow.

fairy tale
A traditional children's story that is often about princes, princesses, imaginary creatures, and magic.

fertility
The ability of animals to have babies, and of plants to produce fruit.

folklore
Customs, stories, songs, jokes, and sayings that are handed down from generation to generation.

generation
All the people of about the same age in a family, social group, or country.

god or goddess
An immortal being that is worshipped because of holding power over human life, nature, or the universe.

hieroglyph
In the ancient Egyptian system of writing, a stylized picture or symbol representing a word or sound.

Hinduism
A religion that developed in India, taking the form we recognize by around 500 BCE. A key idea is *dharma*, which means living a good life.

immortal
Living forever.

Jötnar
A group of Norse gods, goddesses, or godlike beings who were often enemies of the Aesir and Vanir.

kami
A god, goddess, or spirit of the Shinto religion.

legendary
Described in a legend, which is a traditional story that cannot be proved to be true.

medieval
Related to the period in European history between around 600 and 1500.

mortal
Not living forever.

mother goddess
A female deity of motherhood, fertility, and—often—the earth.

mummification
A process for treating a dead body so that it does not decay.

myth
A traditional story—about gods, goddesses, and other immortal beings—that explains nature and human life.

mythology
A collection of myths that belong to a particular people, religion, or culture.

Norse
Related to the peoples who lived in Scandinavia (modern-day Norway, Sweden, and Denmark) in ancient and medieval times.

nymph
A female nature spirit in Greek mythology.

Olympian
A god or goddess who lives on Mount Olympus, Greece's highest mountain.

orisha
In Yoruba belief, a kindly spirit that holds an aspect of the supreme god's power.

papyrus
Used in ancient Egypt, a paper-like material made from papyrus plants.

philosophy
A system of ideas for understanding the universe and leading a good life.

prophecy
A statement about what will happen in the future.

Ragnarök
In Norse mythology, a series of events that will end the current worlds.

religion
A system of beliefs and practices involving the worship of one god, many gods and goddesses, or other supernatural powers.

ritual
A set of actions and words, usually carried out as part of a religious ceremony.

sacred
Deserving of respect or worship because of a link with gods, goddesses, or spirits.

sacrifice
To offer a deity something precious, such as the life of an animal.

saying
A short, well-known statement.

scholar
A person who studies a subject closely.

shape-shifter
Someone who can change into the form of animals, plants, or objects.

Shinto
A religion that developed in Japan by around 2,000 years ago, based on belief in immortal beings called *kami* that live in all things.

shrine
A place of worship that is linked with a god, goddess, spirit, or sacred event.

spirit
An immortal being; also the "soul" of a human that is believed by many religions to live on after the body dies.

spiritual
Related to religion or to the human spirit rather than the body.

subarctic
The region just to the south of the Arctic where there are long, cold winters and short, cool summers.

superhuman
Having abilities that are greater than those of ordinary humans.

supernatural
Related to gods, goddesses, spirits, and other forces that cannot be explained by science.

symbol
An object or sign that represents or stands for something else.

temple
A building used for the worship of a god, goddess, or several deities.

traditional
Passed down from generation to generation.

trickster
In mythology, a god, goddess, spirit, or human who has great intelligence and uses it to play tricks and break rules.

Tuatha Dé Danann
A group of gods, goddesses, or immortal beings in Irish mythology.

Vanir
A clan of Norse gods and goddesses.

Vikings
Seafarers from Scandinavia (modern-day Norway, Sweden, and Denmark) who raided and settled across Europe from the 8th to the 11th centuries.

yin and yang
In Chinese philosophy, opposite forces that balance and complete each other.

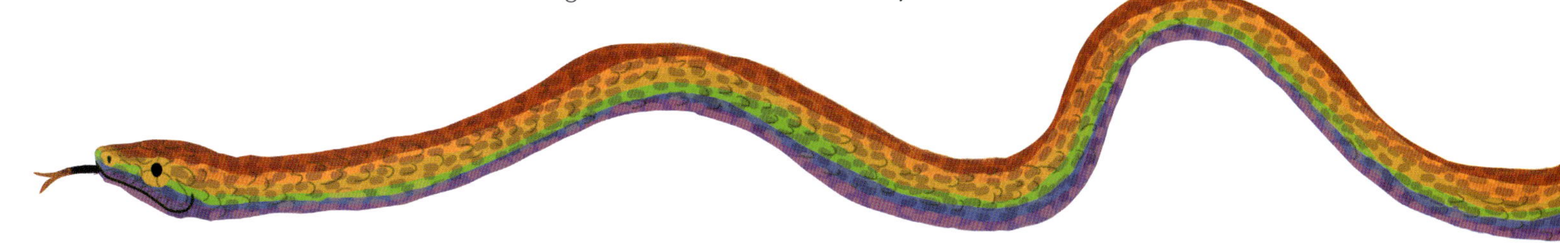

Index